E. Rees

Condensed Chronological History of the Great Rebellion, in the United States

From Nov. 8th., 1860 to May 10th., 1865

E. Rees

Condensed Chronological History of the Great Rebellion, in the United States
From Nov. 8th., 1860 to May 10th., 1865

ISBN/EAN: 9783337187637

Printed in Europe, USA, Canada, Australia, Japan

Cover: Foto ©ninafisch / pixelio.de

More available books at **www.hansebooks.com**

CONDENSED
CHRONOLOGICAL HISTORY

OF THE

GREAT REBELLION,

IN THE

UNITED STATES,

From Nov. 8th, 1860 to May 10th, 1865.

GIVING THE FORCES, BY WHOM LED, DESCRIPTION OF BATTLES, BOMBARDMENTS, SKIRMISHES, SIEGES, RESULTS—NUMBERS KILLED, WOUNDED, PRISONERS OR MISSING ON BOTH SIDES, EXHIBITING IN A CLEAR AND CONCISE MANNER ALL IMPORTANT TRANSACTIONS AND EVENTS OF EACH DAY. ALSO, A SUMMARY GIVING THE NUMBER OF MEN EACH STATE FURNISHED—AGGREGATE AMOUNT OF KILLED AND WOUNDED—TOTAL EXPENSES OF THE WAR—NUMBER OF BATTLES, SKIRMISHES, SHIPS DESTROYED, &c.

COMPILED AND PUBLISHED BY

E. REES AND C. W. REES, A. M.

SAN FRANCISCO
DEFFEBACH & CO. PRINTERS, CORNER OF SANSOME AND MERCHANT STREETS.

1867.

Entered according to Act of Congress. the eighteenth day of July, in the Year of our Lord eighteen hundred and sixty-seven,

By E. REES and C. W. REES, A. M.

In the Clerk's Office of the District Court for the Northern District of the State of California.

CHRONOLOGICAL HISTORY

OF THE

GREAT REBELLION

IN THE

UNITED STATES,

From Nov. 8th. 1860, to May 16th, 1865.

1860.

Nov. 8th. *Presidential Election, returns* stand for A. Lincoln, Republican, 1,857,610; votes, for Stephen A. Douglas, Dem. 1,365.976; for John C. Breckenridge, Dem. 847,953; for John Bell, Union, 590,631. Lincoln's majority over Douglas, 491,634; over Breckenridge, 1.009,657; over Bell, 1,266,979. Mr. Lincoln carries 18 States, Breckenridge 11, Bell 3, Douglas, 2—giving Lincoln 180 Electoral votes, Breckenridge 72, Bell 39, Douglas 12. Lincoln's majority over all, 57.

17th. Grand gathering of citizens of Charleston, S. C., to inaugurate the revolution. The Palmetto flag unfurled, from a fine pole, 100 feet high.

18th. Georgia Legislature appropriates $1,000,000 to arm and equip the State.

20th. Vast quantities of arms for the South arriving in N. Y.

23d. Great public meeting in New Orleans, to organize a "Southern Rights' Association," to carry the State out of the Union.

27th. Gov. Hicks of Maryland, refuses to convene the Legislature and "takes strong ground against Secession."

29th. Dispatches from New Orleans state: "Abolitionists are daily arrested—immense excitement, and the secession feeling momentarily increasing. Disunion is inevitable!"

Dec. 1st. Immense secession meeting at Memphis, Tenn. Pass resolutions accepting the "irrepressible conflict."

Leading citizens of Texas petition Gov. Houston to assemble the Legislature. He refuses.

7th. Buchanan determines to send no more troops to the forts near Charleston, to give no pretext for hostility.

9th. Gov. Brown, of Georgia, publishes a letter favoring immediate secession.

10th. Howell Cobb, Sec. of the Treasury, resignes, having declared himself unable to extricate the treasury from its present bankrupt condition.

Extra session of the Louisiana Legislature meets, passes a military bill appropriating $500,000 to arm the State.

13th. Immense Union Demonstration in Philadelphia.

Mr. Cass, Sec. of State, and Mr. Yancey, Sec. of Navy, strenuously urge the strengthening of Maj. Anderson, but are opposed by President Buchanan.

14th. Lewis Cass resigns his seat in the Cabinet.

25th. Floyd having ordered from the Pittsburg Arsenal, 78 guns to Newport, Texas, and 46 to the Ship Island, at the mouth of the Mississippi, the removal is resisted by the citizens.

18th. Mr. Crittenden's Compromise Resolutions introduced into the U. S. Senate, to renew the Missouri Compromise Line of 1819-21, prohibiting slavery in the territories north of 36 degrees, 30 minutes, and protecting it south of that latitude.... Ordinance of Secession passed by South Carolina. Immense enthusiasm throughout the South.... The Methodist Conference of South Carolina pass resolutions favoring secession.

23d. A defalcation is discovered in the Office of the Interior, of $30,000 from the Indian Trust Fund. Floyd, Sec. of War, implicated.

26th. Maj. Anderson moves by night from Fort Moultrie to Fort Sumter. Causes intense excitement throughout the cotton States. The military in Charleston ordered out. Georgia, Mississippi, Alabama and Florida tender troops.

28th. South Carolina authorities seize the Custom House, Post Office, Arsenal, Castle Pinckney, and Fort Moultrie, occupied by State troops...... A member of the Cabinet at Washington telegraphed : "Troops are pouring in from all directions ; the Palmetto flag waves in triumph !"

1861.

Jan. 1st. Washington City regarded in danger of seizure.

2d. Gen. Scott places the militia of the District under arms, and orders Regulars to the Navy Yard.

Election returns from Georgia show that the State has voted (see figures for and against,) largely for immediate secession. State troops also proceed to take possession of Forts Pulaski and Jackson.... Gov. Ellis, of North Carolina, dispatches troops to seize Fort Macon, at Beaufort, the forts at Wilmington, and the U.

S. Arsenal at Fayetteville....Gov. Pickens, of South Carolina, offered 10,000 troops from without the State.

1,000 negroes are erecting fortifications at Charleston. Channels leading to Fort Sumter obstructed by sunken vessels and the buoys removed.

4th. U. S. Arsenal at Mobile seized by secessionists, having 300,-000 rounds of cartridges, 1,500 barrels of powder; also, Fort Morgan, at the entrance of Mobile Bay.

5th. Several Northern citizens enrolling volunteers to be offered to the President; also, immense Union meetings in Philadelphia and Cincinnati, demanding the President to enforce the laws in all parts of the Union.....The "Star of the West" sailed secretly from New York, with supplies and 250 troops for Fort Sumter.

7th. Alabama and Mississippi Conventions meet; also, the Tennessee and Virginia Legislatures.

8th. Large orders for arms are being filled in N. Y., and Philadelphia for the South.

9th. The "Star of the West" fired into from Fort Moultrie and Morris' Island, and driven back.....The Mississippi Convention passed the ordinance of secession by a vote of 84 to 15.

10th. The Florida Convention passed the ordinance of secession by a vote of 62 to 7. This State cost $5,000,000 in 1820, and the wars of 1818 and 1840 $80,000,000 more.

11th. The Alabama Convention passes the ordinance of secession by a vote of 61 to 39.

The Louisiana authorities seize the arsenal at Baton Rouge, Forts Jackson and St. Phillip, at the mouth of the Mississippi river, and Fort Pike, at Lake Ponchartrain entrance.

New York Legislature tenders the President of the United States aid in support of the Constitution and Union.

13th. The Navy Yard and Ft. Barrancas, Pensacola, surrendered to Florida and Alabama troops.

14th. South Carolina Legislature passes an act that "any attempt by the Federal Government to reinforce Fort Sumter, will be regarded as an open act of hostility, and a declaration of war."

16th. The Crittenden Resolutions lost in the U. S. Senate, by adopting Mr. Clark's substitute, "That the Constitution is good enough, and only wants to be obeyed; that secession is a dangerous remedy, against which all the energies of government should be directed.

18th. The Massachusetts Legislature tenders the President of the United States men and money, to maintain the authority of the General Government.

Virginia Legislature appropriates $1,000,000 for State defense.

19th. Georgia Legislature passed a secession ordinance 208 to 89.

24th. The arsenal at Augusta, Georgia, seized by State authority.

26th. Louisiana State Convention, passed an ordinance of secession by 113 to 17. This State cost the United States $15,000,000.

Feb. 1st. The U. S. Mint and Custom House seized in New Orleans by the State authorities, including $511,000.

Texas Convention passes an ordinance of secession by 166 to 7. This State cost the Government $200,000,000, and the lives of thousands of her brave sons in the Mexican war.

4th. The Congress of the seceded States meets at Montgomery, Alabama.

5th. Peace Convention assembles in Washington.

8th. The Southern Congress adopts a Provisional Constitution.

9th. Jefferson Davis, of Mississippi, is elected President, and Alexander H. Stephens, of Georgia, Vice-President of the " Confederate States of North America."

11th. Mr. Lincoln, President-elect, starts for Washington.

12th. Tennessee returns indicate over 20,000 against a State Convention.

18th. Jefferson Davis inaugurated President of the Confederate States of America, with imposing ceremonies.

23d. Brigadier Gen. Twiggs, of the Texas Department, turnes over all U. S. property to secessionists, worth $1,209,000.

March 2d. Texans seizes the U. S. Revenue Cutter "Dodge," at Galveston.

4th. Inauguration of Abraham Lincoln, the 16th President of the United States. An immense concourse in attendance.

The Confederate flag, with seven stars, unfurled from the Confederate capitol.... Mr. Lincoln's message pronounced a "war declaration," at Montgomery.... Arkansas State Convention meets and elects Union officers by six majority.

Salutes are fired in most Northern cities in honor of the Inauguration and character of Lincoln's Address.

General Beauregard ordered to the chief command at Charleston.

The slaver Bonita is "taken" by Governor Brown and armed as the first ship of Georgia's navy.

The State (Va.) Armory is turning out from 7,000 to 8,000 rifles and musket cartridges per day.

March 5th. A public reception is given in New Orleans to General Twiggs, in honor of his treason.

Mr. Lincoln's Inaugural Message is looked upon with great favor and regarded as a peace offering by the free States, while the Secessionists in the South and their allies in the North see war in the Executive's view of duty to enforce the laws.

6th. Fort Brown, Texas, surrendered to the C. S.

7th. The Louisiana State Convention transfers $536,000 United States gold to the Confederacy.

General Bragg dispatched to Pensacola to assume chief command.

8th. The Confederate Congress calls 50,000 troops into the field for immediate service.

The Missouri Senate instructs her Senators and Congressmen to oppose granting supplies of men and money to coerce the seceded States.

9th. Alabama State Convention turns over all arms, forts, munitions, etc., amounting to ———, seized from the United States, to the Confederate Government.

13th. The Georgia Convention turns over all forts, arsenals, arms, etc., valued at ———, to the Confederacy.

The Charleston (S. C.) Courier, estimates that 3,000 highly disciplined troops are in the various fortifications around the city, and to reinforce Fort Sumter an impossibility.

Seats of United States Senators from the seceded States declared vacant, and their names stricken from the roll.

15th. Mr. Seward, Secretary of State, refuses to recognize the Confederate Commissioners.

16th. Governor Houston, of Texas, refusing to take the oath under the State Constitution, the office of Governor is declared vacant......The Confederate Congress adjourns.

Arizona is voted out of the Union by a Convention of about twenty persons at Mesilla.

18th. Members of the Texas House and Senate take the oath of allegiance to the new government.

20th. The Arkansas Convention adjourns, having refused to pass an Ordinance of Secession....Sloop "Isabel" seized at Mobile by Alabamians, as the first of the war.

21st. Ohio State Legislature asks Congress to call a National Convention.

22d. The Missouri Convention adjourns without passing a Secession Ordinance...A. H. Stephens, in a speech at Savannah, declares that slavery is to be the "chief corner-stone of the new edifice."

April 6th. Major Anderson refuses communication with Charleston by General Beauregard.

8th. Lieutenant Talbot arrives in Charleston to give notice that Major Anderson would be provisioned at all hazards. All Charleston rushes to arms....The Secretary of State announces a peaceful policy to the Confederate Commissioners, declaring a purpose to defend only when assailed.

9th. A dispatch says: Government designs peaceful, unarmed ships to supply United States forts with provisions, troops, etc. If assaulted, the responsibility of inaugurating war must rest with the assailants.

Jefferson Davis calls for 3,500 troops for immediate service from each seceded State, except Florida, 1,500.

10th. Troops drilling in Washington, and additional forces of regulars ordered to the Capitol.

A Charleston dispatch says: "Troops are pouring in from the interior, and all is in readiness for a collision. Fort Sumter will be attacked without waiting for the Abolition fleet—eagerness for the conflict is unbounded. About 7,000 troops are in the defences, with as many more in reserve."

P. Walker, Confederate Secretary of War, orders General Beauregard to demand the evacuation of Fort Sumter; if refused, to reduce the fort.

12th. At 1 o'clock A. M. General Beauregard makes a proposition to Major Anderson if he will name a day to evacuate Fort Sumter, he will not fire on him. Anderson agrees to evacuate on the 15th if not supplied, or does not receive different instructions in the meantime from Washington.

General Beauregard, at 3 o'clock A. M. informs Anderson that the batteries would open on him in one hour from that time.

At 4:30 A. M. Edmund Ruffin fires the first gun on Fort Sumter, garrisoned with 80 men, followed by all the batteries. Anderson returns the fire soon after daylight, the engagement terrific on both sides...... Walker, Secretary of War, serenaded in honor of the bombardment, says, by the 1st of May the Confederate flag will float over the dome of the Capitol at Washington, and may yet float over Fanueil Hall in Boston.... Five millions of dollars appropriated for arming the military of Pennsylvania by the Legislature.

13th. Bombardment of Fort Sumter continues—barracks on fire—flames become general—men stifled by intense heat and smoke—hot shot and shell pouring into the fort—the magazine explodes—fire spreads to the gates—the fort fast becoming a ruin—the flag staff shot down, but replaced—yet Anderson refuses to surrender only on his first proposal.

14th. Anderson evacuates Fort Sumter, with five wounded, to a force under General Beauregard of 7,000. The news of the bombardment electrifies the entire North—immense excitement—both State authorities and the humble individual hastens to support the insulted Government and flag—there is but one prevailing sentiment, that Government is right and shall be sustained whatever the sacrifice.

15th. President Lincoln issues a proclamation, announcing an insurrection in the seven seceded States too powerful for suppression by the ordinary Courts and Marshals, and therefore calls out 75,000 militia.

16th. Governors of Tennessee, Missouri, Virginia, and Kentucky refuse to furnish their quota of troops as called for by President Lincoln.

Excitement in the North becomes more intense—great satisfac-

tion expressed by all classes at the course of the Administration—the free States respond with money and men to the President's call....Jeff. Davis calls for 32,500 troops, making 75,000 in all.
Fort Pickens reinforced and re-provisioned by United States transports.
Several Pennsylvania military companies reach Washington, first on the roll of honor, in response to the President's call.

17th. The Sixth Massachusetts State Militia leaves for Washington. the first complete regiment to respond to the call.
The Virginia State Convention passes an Ordinance of Secession by 60 to 53, in secret session.

18th. Major Anderson reaches New York—is the hero of the day....The Star of the West is seized at Indianola, Texas.

19th. Harper's Ferry armory and public store houses burnt by the United States guard to prevent their falling into rebel hands.
Attack on Sixth Massachusetts Regiment by the Baltimore mob, 2 soldiers killed, 11 wounded, and one mortally; 11 of the mob killed, and four wounded—the city all in arms....U. S. President announces a blockade of the ports in all rebellious States.

20th. Grand Union demonstration in New York city—60,000 citizens of all parties and classes participate......Gosport Navy Yard burned by order of Macauley, commanding; $11,000,000 worth of property destroyed....C. S. seize the Branch Mint at Charlotte, N. C....Mob law in Baltimore; Arsenal at Liberty, Mo., seized; Fortress Monroe reinforced.

21st. Thousands of "war sermons" preached in Northern cities, inspiring the public mind to trust in God and to energetic patriotism.

22d. U. S. arsenals seized at Fayetteville, N. C., and at Napoleon, Arkansas....Grand Union demonstration in Lexington, Ky.

23d. Martial law proclaimed in Baltimore.
The first S. C. regiment starts for the North.

25th. Fort Smith, Arkansas, seized....Extra session of the Kentucky Legislature called.....Major Sibley, of the U. S. Army surrenders 450 United States troops to the Confederates "upon demand," at Saluria, Texas....The New York Seventh reaches Washington, and the capital regarded safe.....Governor Letcher proclaims Virginia annexed to the confederacy without the vote of the people... United States Senator Douglas declares for the Union and support of the Administration, and enforcing the laws.

26th. Governor Brown, of Georgia, orders all debts due in free States paid into the State Treasury.

27th. 21,000 troops reported in Washington; the enemy also concentrating to menace the capital.

29th. Maryland Legislature votes against secession.
The Confederate Congress meets in extra session.
Indiana votes $500,000 to arm her troops.

May 1st. N. C., Legislature passes the State Convention bill.

3d. President Lincoln calls for 42,000 volunteers; 22,000 for the regular army, and 18,000 seamen; making in all 117,000 troops.

Fourteen Kentucky companies offer their services to the U.S. Gove

Connecticut Legislature votes $2,000,000 for war purposes.

4th. Governors of Western and Middle States convene in Cleveland, Ohio, for consultation.

5th. The "day of grace," allotted by President Lincoln, for the returning of those in rebellion expires.... Confederate Congress declares war existing with the United States.

6th. Virginia admitted into the Southern Confederacy by secret session of the C. S. Congress. Seventeen days after this the people permitted to vote on the ordinance.

Arkansas State Convention passes a Secession Ordinance by 69 to 1, and not submitted to the people.

Privateering by the Confederate Government sanctioned.

Tennessee Legislature passes a "declaration of independence," to be submitted to the people June 8th.

7th. Governor Harris, of Tennessee, announces a "league" with the Confederate States, which places the State under C. S. control and awes Unionists into submission.

Union meeting and United States flag raised at Knoxville, Tenn.

8th. The Governor of Ohio calls for 100,000 troops.

10th. Major-General R. E. Lee, of Virginia, late Colonel in the United States army, appointed to command the army of Virginia.

General Lyon captures Camp Jackson near St. Louis, with 639 prisoners, and many arms and munitions of war, thus preventing the State from being forced out of the Union.

11th. Union troops being again assailed in St. Louis, killed four of the mob.... Great Union demonstration in San Francisco.

Charleston harbor blockaded.

13th. Brigadier-General Butler occupies Federal Hill, Baltimore, opening the road to Washington.

Delegates from 35 counties meet at Wheeling, Va., and repudiate the Act of Secession and propose a division of the State on the line of the Blue Ridge.... Mississippi river blockaded at Cairo.

Queen Victoria issues a proclamation of neutrality.

14th. Governor Hicks calls for Maryland's quota of U. S. troops.

15th. Massachusetts Legislature offers to loan $7,000,000 to the Federal Government.... Harper's Ferry fortified by Confederates.

17th. C. S. Congress authorizes $50,000,000 bonds issued bearing 3 per cent., and payable in 20 years, and $20,000,000 treasury notes, without interest.

All communication with the South prohibited.

18th. Arkansas admitted into the Confederacy.

United States gunboats dislodge a C. S. battery at Sewell's

Point, Va., the first naval operation of the war.

20th. Governor Magoffin proclaims Kentucky's "neutrality."

21st. North Carolina State Convention passes an Ordinance of Secession..... The Repudiation Act of the C. S. Congress signed by Jeff. Davis, by which all dues to Northern creditors must be paid into the Confederate treasury.

William McSpedon and Samuel Smith, of New York, capture the first Confederate flag at Alexandria.

Confederate Congress adjourns to meet in Richmond.

24th. 13,000 Union troops pass into Virginia commanding Arlington Hights and the Potomac from Alexandria to Georgetown.

Colonel Ellsworth is shot in the Marshall House, Alexandria, while returning from the dome with a rebel flag, by James Jackson, who is also instantly shot.

General Butler moves from Fortress Monroe into Virginia.

26th. Western Virginia votes overwhelmingly for the Union.

27th. Major-General Butler "receives over 100 runaway negroes," declares them "contraband of war," and is sustained by the War Department and the President.... Mobile blockaded.

28th. Savannah blockaded. Union troops occupy Newport News

29th. Jeff Davis arrives in Richmond.

Enthusiastic Union Meeting at Paris, France,

Grafton, Va., taken by Union troops.

Lieut. Tompkins makes a gallant dash into the Confederate lines at Fairfax Court House with 75 mounted men. Union loss, 1 killed, 1 missing, and four wounded. Confederate loss, 10 killed and wounded, and 5 prisoners.... Capt. Lyon commissioned Brig. General, and supersedes Harney in Missouri.

June 1st. All U. S. postal facilities suspended in the seceded States.... Jeff. Davis addresses the people of Richmond, and calls Lincoln "an ignorant usurper."

Gunboats "Freeborn" and "Anacosta" silence the batteries on Aquia Creek.

3d. 5,000 Ohio and Indiana troops under Col.'s Kelly and Lander, defeat 1,500 Confederates at Phillippi, Va., under Porterfield. Union loss, 2 killed, 2 wounded and 2 missing. Confederate loss, 16 killed and 10 prisoners.

U. S. Senator Douglas dies at Chicago; his last words a message to his children to "obey the laws and support the Constitution of the United States."

Border State Convention meets at Frankfort, Ky.

Gen. Beauregard takes command of the Confederate Army headquarters at Manassas Junction.

6th. The gunboat "Harriet Lane" encounters the C. S. batteries at Pig Point, Va., with but little result.

8th. Convention ratifies the Confederate Constitution.

Major General Patterson moves from Chambersburg toward Harper's Ferry *via* Hagarstown.

10th. The enemy, 2,200 strong, under Magruder, are attacked by 3,000 Federals, under Brig. Gen. Pierce, in their strongly fortified position at Big Bethel, Va. Union troops compelled to retire, after an obstinate but badly conducted action of two hours. Union loss, killed 16, wounded 35, missing 6. Here the gallant Lieut Greble and Major T. Winthrop fell.

Gen. Banks takes command of the Department of Annapolis.

11th. Col. Lew Wallace, commanding the Indiana Zouaves, drives 600 Confederates out of Romney, Va.

Wheeling Constitutional Convention meets.

13th. Confederate day of fasting and prayer.

14th. Harper's Ferry evacuated by the enemy, after destroying all the public works and immense amount of other property.

Gov. Jackson leaves Jefferson City, Mo.

15th. Gen. Lyon occupies Jefferson City, Mo.

The enemy gathering under Gen. Price at Boonville, Mo.

16th. Skirmish at Seneca Mills ; 3 Confederates killed.

17th. Western Virginia resolves upon a separate State.

Federal troops attacked by a mob in St. Louis ; 6 rioters killed, and others wounded.

At Vienna, Virginia, the enemy fire into a railroad train of 697 Ohio troops, under Gen. Schenck, killing 8 and wounding 12.

BATTLE OF BOONVILLE, Mo.—Gen. Lyon, with 1,500 men, routs 2,000 Confederates under Gen. Price and Gov. Jackson, capturing much plunder and killing 25, wounding 50 ; Unionists, 2 killed, 9 wounded, 20 missing.

18th. Edward's Ferry skirmish, 1 killed; enemy's loss unknown·

President Lincoln receives the first message ever sent from a balloon as to military movements.

BATTLE OF CAMP COLE, Mo.—800 loyal Home Guards, but partially armed, under Captain Cooke, are defeated by 400 Confederates under Gov. Jackson, who lost 4 killed and 40 wounded; Unionists, 25 killed, 75 wounded and taken prisoners.

19th. The Cherokee Chief, John Ross, urges neutrality on his Nation ....35 Confederates captured at Liberty, Missouri, with valuable stores....The enemy occupy Piedmont. Va.

20th. Major General McClellan takes command in Western Virginia ... War Department and field movements first connected by telegraph....Frank H. Pierpont, a strong Union man, elected Governor of Western Virginia by the Wheeling Convention.

21st. East Tennessee Union Convention oppose secession.

23d. The enemy destroy 48 locomotives, shops, machinery, etc., belonging to the Baltimore & Ohio Railroad, at Martinsburg, Va., valued at $400,000.

24th. Governor Harris proclaims Tennessee out of the Union. Declaring 104,019 having voted for secession, and 47,238 against. Virginia is announced to have voted 128,884 for secession, 32,134 against. In both States (Tenn. and Va.,) the election was conducted under rebel bayonets, and all timid Union men deterred from voting.

25th. Iowa Legislature votes $600,000 for the war.

26th. The President of the United States acknowledges the government instituted by the Wheeling Convention as the *de facto* Government of Virginia.

13 Indiana Zouaves defeates 41 rebels at Patterson Creek, Va., Unionists, 1 killed, 1 wounded; rebels, 8 killed. 17 horses captured, when the rebels being reinforced by about 70, made second attack, when 23 of them fell.

27th. The gunboats " Pawnee " and " Freeborn " engage the rebel batteries at Mathias' Point, Va., Capt. Wood killed, and 8 seamen wounded.

A large East Tennessee Convention assembled at Knoxville, and protests against the acts of violence by which Tennessee was given into the hands of the Southern Confederacy, and claims the State yet in the Union.

28th. Skirmishing at Fall's Church and Shooter's Hill, Va., and at Cumberland and Wheeler Gaps, East Tenn.

29th. Grand Council of War in Washington.

July 1st. Capt Semmes, with the privateer "Sumter," escapes from the Mississippi river.

Confederates routed at Buckhannon, Va., with 23 killed and wounded, and 200 prisoners. Skirmish at Farmington, Mo., 5 rebels killed, 2 prisoners.

BATTLE OF MARTINSBURG, VA.—5,000 Confederates under Gen. Johnston defeated by 15,000 under Gen. Patterson, and pursued 2 miles. Unionists 3 killed and 10 wounded; Confederates 31 killed and 50 wounded.

2d. The new Virginia Legislature organized at Wheeling.

3d. A company of 94 Confederates captured at Neosho, Mo.

4th. U. S. Congress meets in extra session, present only A. Johnson from Tennessee, and 3 Virginia Representatives, from the 11 seceded States.

The President in his message, calls for 400,000 volunteers, and $400,000,000 to crush the rebellion.

5th. The opposition in Congress reduced to 6 Senators and 5 Representatives.

BATTLE OF CARTHAGE, Mo.—Col. Sigel, skirmishing with 1,600 men, came in contact with 3,500 men under Price, Gov. Jackson, Rains and Parsons. Sigel, after hours of gallant resistance, retires slowly, dealing a heavy blow to the enemy at each retiring step.

U. S. loss, 13 killed, 31 wounded. C. S. loss, 80 killed, 110 wound.
6th. Department of the West created, and Fremont placed in command.
45 men of the 3d Ohio, on a scout, cut their way through 250 Confederates at Middle York Bridge, Va.
8th. Confederates lose 3 killed and 28 wounded in a skirmish at Bird's Point, Mo...At Bealington, Va., enemy routed....Enemy's camp at Florida, Mo., broken up....President Lincoln, by flag of truce, receives dispatches threatening retaliation if any privateers are hung.
10th. McClellan's advance, after several hours' battle, routs the enemy at Lawrel Hill, Va.
After severe fighting the enemy are driven from Monroe Station, Mo., losing 75 prisoners and one gun.
11th. Colonel Pegram being intrenched with 800 troops at Rich Mountain, Va., is surprised and attacked by the 8th, 10th, 13th Indiana, and 19th Ohio regiments, under General Rosecrans. After a hard fought battle, the enemy are driven from the intrenchments and retreat, sustaining a loss of 60 killed, many wounded and prisoners, and all his camp equipage. United States loss, 11 killed, and 35 wounded.
United States Senate expels the members from Virginia, North Carolina, Texas, Arkansas, and Nicholson from Tennessee.
12th. Skirmish at Barboursville, West Virginia....Two Union regiments organized in New Mexico....Skirmish near Newport News, the enemy capturing 12 United States troops.
13th. BATTLE OF CARRICK'S FORD, VA.—McClellan's advance of 2,000 men, under Gen. Morris and Capt. Benham, engaged 3,000 rebels under Gen. Garnett. Garnett was killed, his troops routed with 20 killed, 10 wounded and 50 missing; U.S. loss, 2 killed and 12 wounded....600 Confederates strongly posted at Barboursville, Va., are driven out at the point of the bayonet by 300 United States troops of Colonel Woodruff's command.
15th. General Patterson's advance routes 600 Confederate cavalry at Bunker Hill, Va.
16th. The Army of the Potomac advances toward Centreville and Manassas.
17th. Enemy driven back with loss in a skirmish at Fulton, Mo. General McDowell's advance occupy Fairfax Court House.
U. S. troops are repulsed with 30 killed & wounded at Scarztown.
18th. General Tyler encounters Beauregard's right advance in a strong position at Blackburn Ford, on Bull Run. After a severe conflict, Tyler, being ordered not to bring on a general engagement, falls back to Centreville to await the arrival of the main army. United States loss, 19 killed, 38 wounded, 26 missing. Confederates 15 killed, 53 wounded.

General Patterson is under strict orders to engage Johnson's forces at Winchester, at all hazards, but in place of this he moves his entire army from Bunker Hill to Charlestown, Va., off from the Winchester road, permitting Johnston to escape.

19th. Patterson superseded by General Banks for not engaging Johnston..... General Dix takes Banks' command.

20th. Confederates under General Wise retire up the Kanawha Valley, Va... Confederate Congress meets at Richmond. Intense anxiety felt as to the fate of the Confederate army at Bull Run and Manassas.... Johnston ordered to reinforce Beauregard.

21st. BATTLE OF BULL RUN.—General McDowell with 55,000 troops, hurls 18,000 against 21,833 Confederates under General Beauregard. After three desperate charges of five hours duration, the enemy are driven back one and a half miles and disappear, and Beauregard decides to fall back to Manassas; victory now perches on the brow of the loyal army. At this juncture the enemy are reinforced by Johnson's army of 5,167 from Winchester, which Patterson had permitted to escape and increase the enemy's force engaged to 27,000. This decides the day against the Union forces, which being composed mainly of raw material, are precipitated into a disorderly retreat and flee from the bloody field. United States loss 481 killed, 1,011 wounded, 1,216 missing, 17 pieces of artillery, 150 boxes of small arm cartridges, 87 boxes of rifle-cannon ammunition, 30 boxes of old fire-arms, 13 wagon loads of provisions, 2,500 muskets, 8,000 knapsacks, blankets, etc. Enemies loss, 269 killed, 1,483 wounded. While the result of this battle served as an opiate to the South, it most effectually aroused every latent power of the North; she prepared and marshaled on those terrible fields of strife that followed, such imposing columns as finally bore down all opposition......McClellan appointed to the command of the Army of the Potomac..... Great excitement, mortification, and indignation felt throughout the loyal States at the Bull Run disaster ... Colonel Sweeny disperses a band of rebels at Forsyth, Mo., killing 5.

24th. Lieutenant Crosby, dashing up Rock River, Va., burns 9 vessels and seizes one as a prize.

25th. General Rosecrans assigned to the command of Western Virginia..... General Cox occupies Charlestown, Va., and Wise retreats up the river....General Fremont takes command at St. Louis....General Banks takes command at Harper's Ferry.

26th. Enemy repulsed at Lane's Prairie, Mo.

28th. General Thanksgiving in the Confederacy for Manassas victory.

29th. Four Union gunboats engage a battery planted at Aquia Creek, on the Potomac.

Wise flees up the Kanawha to escape Cox's pursuit.

30th. The Missouri State Convention declares the offices of Governor, Lieutenant-Governor, and Secretary of State vacant.

August 1st. Secretary of War orders all negroes in the Union lines, or such as may came in, to be employed on military works.

2d. Congress passes a bill providing for 500,000 men.

Battle of Dug Springs, Mo.—General Lyon with 5,000 loyalists defeats General Price. Union loss, 8 killed, and 30 wounded, Rebels, 40 killed, and 44 wounded....Fort Fillmore, New Mexico, with 750 men, betrayed by its commander, Major Lynn....Unionists destroy the enemies vessels and stores in Pokomoke Sound.

3d. Congressional Act confiscating all slaves used by rebels for military purposes.

5th. Galveston blockaded......Enemy defeated at Athens, Mo. Skirmish at Point of Rocks, Virginia.

7th. The rebel General Magruder burns Hampton, Va. United States gunboat "Union" burns the privateer "York."

8th. Enemy routed at Lovettsville, Va.

9th. At Potosi, Mo., enemy defeated—30 killed and wounded.

10th. BATTLE OF WILSON'S CREEK, Mo.—General Lyon with 6,000 men attacks the enemy 23,000 strong, commanded by McCulloch, Price and Raines. One of the bloodiest battles of the war ensues, in which the immortal Lyon falls while leading his men in a bayonet charge. His forces now fall back to Springfield, and then in good order retreat to Rolla. Union loss 223 killed, 721 wounded, 291 missing. Rebel loss, killed 265, wounded 800, missing, 30.

12th. Gen. Wool appointed to the command of Fortress Monroe.

13th. Union troops occupy Grafton, Va....Skirmish at Mathias' Point, Va., Union loss 3 killed, 1 wounded ; rebel loss, 21.

14th. Fremont declares martial law in St. Louis.

Jeff. Davis notifies all in the Confederacy, not recognizing its authority, to leave within 40 days.

16th. The President of the United States orders all commercial intercourse between the loyal and seceded States to cease.

Colonel Hecker surprises a rebel camp at Frederickstown, Mo.

18th. The rebels sustain loss at Lady's Fork, Va.

19th. Several newspapers mobbed in the Northern States for disloyalty....Union troops retake Commerce, Missouri.

20th. Enemy, 4,000 strong, assault the Eleventh Ohio, at Hawks' Nest, Va. ; are repulsed with a loss of 50 ; Union loss, 2 killed.

The enemy driven out of Charleston, Mo., with 40 killed, and 17 prisoners; Union loss, 1 killed, 6 wounded.

The Wheeling Convention creates Western Virginia a State.

21st. Skirmish at Cross Lanes, Va.

22d. New York city disloyal newspapers denied the use of the mails, by order of the Postmaster-General.

24th. Governor Gamble calls for 42,000 troops for State service, and to repel the enemy from Missouri.

26th. The Fourth Ohio, surprised while at breakfast by 3,000 infantry, 400 cavalry, and 10 guns, under Floyd. The Ohioans with coolness form in line of battle, and fight till nearly out-flanked, then charge, cutting their way through the enemy's ranks, and are not pursued.

28th. The Hatteras, N. C., expedition under General B. F. Butler, 1,000 strong, and the fleet under Com. S. H. Stringham, bombards Forts Hatteras and Clark, held by Com. Barron about 800 strong.

29th. After suffering from a most terrific fire from the fleet, Hatteras and Clark capitulates, with 49 killed, 51 wounded, 715 prisoners, (including Com. Barron and 44 officers) 25 32-pounders, 1,000 stand of arms, great quantity of munitions, stores, etc. Union loss, 1 killed and 2 wounded.

Two thousand rebels attack 230 Union troops intrenched at Lexington, Mo., but repulsed with 60 killed.

Twenty-three rebels captured at Greytown, Mo.

30th. Fremont proclaims martial law throughout Missouri.

September 1st. Enemy routed at Boone C. H., Va., by a brilliant charge of Captain Wheeler's command; 11 rebels killed, and 40 prisoners.... Home Guards repulse 250 rebels at Bennett's Mills, Mo.; Union loss, 2 killed, 7 wounded.

2d. Charlestown, Va., Home Guards surrounded near Harper's Ferry by a section of the Thirteenth Massachusetts; enemies loss, 3 killed, 5 wounded, 22 prisoners.... Montgomery attacks the rebel General Rains, near Fort Scott, Kansas, and is repulsed.

4th. The rebel General Polk invades Kentucky.

5th. 1,100 Unionists at Shelbind, Mo.. retreat, leaving all their camp equipage to escape capture by Green's rebel command.

6th. General Pope marches against Green's forces at Huntsville, Mo., who flees, leaving his baggage, stores, etc.

7th. The Kentucky House of Representatives vote 77 to 20 to hoist the Federal flag over the State House.

8th. General Grant, with two regiments, occupies Paducah, Ky., in consequence of rebel invasion.

9th. One hundred and fifty Union prisoners ordered to Castle Pinckney, S. C., to be incarcerated as hostages for the safety of the privateers on trial in New York.

10th. BATTLE OF CARNIFEX FERRY, W. Va.—Rosecrans, with 4,500 Unionists, attacks Gen. Floyd's entrenched camp, 5,000 strong, darkness coming on, the Union troops lie on their arms all night and make a combined assault in the morning, but Floyd has fled, leaving his baggage, stores, etc.; loss not reported; Union loss 16 killed, and 102 wounded.

12th. BATTLE OF CHEAT MOUNTAIN, W. Va.—General R. E. Lee, with 9,000 troops, appears before General Reynolds' position with

10,000 men, and surround the loyal troops on the hill, who, on the 13th, pierce the enemies lines, capturing valuable stores. Gen. Reynolds also holds Elkwater against all of Lee's efforts. On the 14th the enemy being disconcerted by Federal tactics, retire with a loss of 80 killed, 20 wounded, and 20 prisoners; Federals, 9 killed, 2 wounded, and 60 prisoners.

Enemies camp at Petersburgh. Va., broken up.... Major Gavitt's cavalry attacks and routs the guerrilla Talbot, near Ironton, Mo.

13th. Leading secessionists in Maryland having formed a conspiracy to "carry the State out of the Union," are arrested ...The rebel Col. Brown attacks 150 Home Guards at Boonville, under Captain Eppstein; Brown is defeated and killed, with 11 others, and 40 wounded.... Enemy's battery silenced on the Potomac, opposite Shepardstown, Va., after heavy cannonading.... The fleet and Newport News camp fired at by the rebel ironclad "Yorktown."

14th. Privateer " Judah " burnt in Pensacola harbor.

15th. Colonel Geary is attacked near Darnstown, Md., by the enemy, who are finally repulsed with loss.

16th. 6,000 rebels under Price attack the intrenched camp at Lexington, Mo., under Colonel Mulligan, who repulses the enemy with heavy loss.... Enemy evacuate Ship Island.

Skirmish at Blue Mills Landing, Mo.

17th. Cols. Montgomery and Johnston, with 600 men, repulse the enemy at Mariatown, Mo., killing 7, and capturing their camp, equipage, stores, etc.

17th-18th. The Home Guard, at Barboursville, Ky., skirmishing with Zollicoffer's scouts, who are finally driven off.

20th. Gen. Mulligan, with 2,780 Unionists, after ho'ding his position 8 days, surrenders his forces to Gen. Price, with 26,000, after sustaining an unremitted assault and bombardment for 59 hours, while all water communication is cut off. Union loss, 42 killed and 108 wounded 1,624 prisoners. Rebel loss, 25 killed, 75 wounded.

21st. Gen. Lanes' troops surprise a superior force of Confederates at Papinsville, Mo. After a severe fight, the enemy retreats, leaving 40 killed, 100 prisoners, their tents, wagons, and supplies.

Gen. Rob't. Anderson assumes command of the Union troops in Kentucky.

23d. Cols. Cantwell and Parke, with one gun and Ringgold's cavalry advance from New Creek, Va., and drive the enemy 700 strong, from Mechanicsburg Gap; then push on into Romney and storm the town, driving 1,400 Confederate infantry and cavalry into the mountains, with a loss of only 28 killed.

25th. The enemy, with 4 regiments, attack the Union troops at Lewisville, Va., and are repulsed.

Col. Pratt's 34th Ohio Zouaves 560 strong, storm the enemy

under Col. F. W. Davis 5,000 strong, and killed 29, wounded 50, and take 47 prisoners, sustaining a loss of 4 killed and nine wounded and missing.

26th. Day of fasting and prayer throughout the loyal States.

27th. Fremont, 12,000 men, leaves St. Louis in pursuit of Price.

28th. Enemy evacuates Munson's Hill.

29th. Price evacuating Lexington, Mo.

Oct. 2d-3d. BATTLE OF GREEN BRIAR, VA.—Gen. Reynolds, with 5,000 Unionists, attacks Gen. Johnson with 7,000 Confederates. After a severe contest of an hour, the enemy retire, with 100 killed, 75 wounded, and 13 prisoners. Union loss, 8 killed and 32 wounded.

3d. The Federals being greatly outnumbered in an engagement at Union Hill, Kentucky, retire, after a stubborn and bloody resistance.

4th. Col. Brown's Federal command at Chicacomico, North Carolina, being attacked, retires under cover of the gunboats, at Hatteras Light House, losing 40 prisoners.

5th. With great slaughter, the gunboat "Monticello" shells the enemy at Chilicomico.

8th. Gen. W. T. Sherman takes command in Kentucky, Gen. Anderson retiring on account of ill health.

50 Home Guards, in a gallant engagement near Hillsboro, Ky., defeat a large body of Confederates, killing 11, wounding 29, and taking 22 prisoners, and losing but 3 killed, and 2 wounded.

Grand Review of the Army of the Potomac.

9th--10th. The rebels, 2,000 strong, under Gen. Anderson, attacke Col. W. Wilson's Zouave camp of 400, and are repulsed after an obstinate fight. U. S. loss, 14 killed. 29 wounded, and 24 missing; rebel loss, unknown, wounded 350, and prisoners 36.

12th. Enemy attack the Mississippi blockading fleet, but driven back.... Union Convention in Hyde county, N. C.

13th. Major Wright's cavalry defeat 300 rebels near Lebanon, Mo., killing 20 and taking 30 prisoners, and losing but one man.

The Unionists defeat the rebels near Bird's Point, Mo., but in a second engagement, are overpowered by superior numbers.

14th. Major Wright's cavalry capture 45 guerillas, and the notorious Bill Robbins, at Lynn Creek, Mo.

16th. Capt. Geary passes into Virginia at Harper's Ferry, with 400 Unionists, and captures 21,000 bushels of wheat; is fiercely assailed at Bolivar and London Heights, defeats his antagonists, and arrives safely at the Maryland shore, losing 4 killed and 8 wounded.... Major White's Prairie Scouts, 150 strong, dash into Lexington, Mo.. capture the garrison of 306 rebels, stores, arms, etc. .... Enemies pronounce the Potomac blockaded.

17th. Major Gavitt's command routs a large rebel force after a gallant fight near Frederickton, Mo..... Lieut. Kirby defeats the rebels near Lime Creek, Missouri, killling 5.

Col. Morgan's 18th Missouri, routs the enemy in a conflict at Big Hurricane Creek, Missouri, killing 14, and taking 8 prisoners ; Union loss, 14 wounded, 2 mortally.

21st. BATTLE OF BALL'S BLUFF.—Union troops under Col. Baker, 2,100 strong, engage 5,000 of the enemy under Gen. Evans, at Ball's Bluff. After hours of the most daring and gallant fighting, the eloquent and patriotic Baker falls, while leading his brave men up in the face of death. The Federals struggle on, but are defeated, and retreat closely pursued to the river, and not finding sufficient transports in readiness, are shot down like wild beasts, as they scatter along the stream or attempt to swim the river ; 223 killed, 266 wounded, and 455 missing. Enemy's loss, 36 killed, 264 wounded, 2 prisoners.

The rebels, 2,500 strong, under Jeff. Thompson and Col. Lowe, are attacked at Fredericktown, Mo., by Col. Plummer ; after two hours severe contest, the enemy flee in disorder, and are pursued for twenty-two miles. Col. Lowe is slain, and 200 killed and wounded : the Union loss is 6 killed and 40 wounded.

Gen. Zoilicoffer, with about 7,500 rebels defeated at Camp Wildcat, Kentucky, by Gen. Schoeff. Union loss, 4 killed and 21 wounded. Rebel loss not known.

22d. Nelson's forces, in two divisions, defeat the enemy at West Liberty, Ky., killing 21, taking 34 prisoners, 52 horses and capturing Hazelgreen with 38 prisoners.

23d. The enemy, 100 strong, are defeated by Lieut. Grayson, with 50 men of the 6th Indiana, near Hodgeville, Ky., with a loss of 3 killed and 5 wounded.

25th. BATTLE OF SPRINGFIELD, Mo.—Major Zagonyi, with 300 men of Fremont's body-guard, and White's Prairie Scouts, dash against 2,000 rebels in line of battle, defeating and driving them out, killing 106, wounding 60, and taking 27 prisoners. Union loss, 15 killed, 27 wounded, and 10 missing.

26th. BATTLE OF ROMNEY, VA.—Gen. Kellogg, with 2,500 men, by a night march attack the enemy. After a determined battle, the enemy are defeated, losing 1,500 prisoners and large quantities of war material. Federal loss, 2 killed and 15 wounded.

300 of the 9th Kansas, under Major Phillips, attack and defeat the enemy at Saratoga, Ky., killing 13, capturing 21 and 52 horses.

27th. The Unionists attack and break up a rebel camp at Plattsburg, Mo., killing 8 and capturing 11.

28th. Lieut. Hopkins, with a gunboat, passes up the Chincoteague Inlet, Va., and burns 3 rebel vessels.

29th. Col. Burbank, with 250 men, and two pieces of artillery, defeats and drives the enemy 400 strong, from Woodbury, capturing their camp, stores, equipage, etc.

History of the Great Rebellion

Port Royal Expedition leaves Fortress Monroe.

Nov. 1st. Gen. Geo. B. McClellan appointed General-in-Chief of the U. S. Army... A large rebel camp surprised and scattered at Renwick, Mo., losing about 50 in killed and wounded, and all their camp equipage, stores, etc.

2d. Gen. Hunter supersedes Gen. Fremont in the Department of the West...:. Major Joseph routs the enemy in an engagement at Platte City, Mo., killing and wounding 14 and capturing 30.

4th. Col. Padge captures a large amount of rebel stores and several prisoners at Harston, Mo.

6th. Rosecrans silences Floyd's batteries on Gauley river.

500 rebels capture 120 Unionists at Little Santa Fe, New Mexico.

7th. BATTLE OF BELMONT, Mo.—Gens. Grant and McClernand, with 2,500 men, advance on the enemy. After a stubborn resistance, the enemy is driven, and his camp burnt. Grant returning, is assailed by a large reinforcement from Columbus, but cuts his way back to his boats. Union loss, 84 killed, 288 wounded, and 235 prisoners. Rebel loss, 261 killed, 427 wounded, & 278 prisoners.

7th. Port Royal Expedition, commanded by Gen. Sherman, 27,000 strong, and fleet of over 70 vessels, commanded by Admiral Dupont, bombards Forts Walker and Beauregard, under General Drayton, at the entrance to Port Royal Harbor; after a terrific contest of five hours, the Forts surrender, and the flag again waves in South Carolina. The fleet lost 8 killed and 23 wounded. Rebel loss about 100 killed and wounded, 2,500 prisoners, and much valuable property.

Beaufort and Hilton Head occupied by Unionists.

8th. Capt. Charles Wilkes, of the "San Jacinto," arrests the Rebel Com's Mason and Slidell, on the British steamer "Trent."

9th. Gen. Halleck ordered to take command in Missouri, and Gen. Buell in Kentucky.

10th. The 9th Va. Union volunteers surprised at Guyandotte, Western Virginia, with near 150 killed and captured.

11th. Col. Anthony, with 100 Kansas troops, defeats a rebel camp after a severe skirmish near Kansas City. Federal loss, 8 killed and 8 wounded. Rebel loss unknown.

The enemy defeated by Col. Max. Weber, in an engagement at Newmarket Bridge, near Fortress Monroe.

12th. A reconnoisance in force from Alexandria to Oscoquan Creek, by Gen. Heintzelman.

13th. Gen. Lockwood leaves Baltimore with a strong Federal column, and occupies the Virginia counties east of the Potomac.

Governor Harris, of Tennessee, authorized to call out 10,000 militia for the Confederacy.

Zollicoffer retreats to Cumberland Gap, Tenn.

14th. General Rosecrans dispatches General Benham to attack

General Floyd's rear—engages his outposts at McCoy's Mills, and defeats the enemy, killing 15, including Colonel Croghan. Floyd's main army escapes south.....A rebel force surprised and 3 killed by Col. Geary, attempting to erect a battery near Point of Rocks.

15th. Confederate fast day.

17th. Colonel Alcorn defeats Hawkins' rebel camp near Rumsey, Ky. taking 25 prisoners, 300 horses. U.S. loss, 10 killed, 15 wounded. Surrender of Port Royal causes a panic in Charleston.

18th. Forty-five counties represented in Convention at Hatteras, N. C., repudiate the State Secession Ordinance.

Fifty recruits for Price captured near Warrenburg, Mo.

About 40 leading Secessionists "with closed doors," pass a Secession Ordinance at Russelville, Ky. .

19th. The rebel privateer "Nashville," burns the ship "Harvey Birch," near Southampton, England....Enemy burns Warsaw, Missouri....Enemy defeated at Wist's Court House, Virginia.

20th. Stone fleet sails from New London and New Bedford, to be sunk in Southern harbors ...General McClellan makes a grand review of his troops before Washington—20,000 spectators....Col. Burchard and 24 men routs the notorious Hayes, near Kansas City.

General Floyd becomes frightened at Gauley River, and flees, leaving all arms, ammunition, and camp equipage.

22d. Federal gunboats shell and destroy a rebel camp above Newport News.

One hundred Kentuckians repulse 500 rebels at Brownsville.

22d-23d. Fort Pickens bombards the rebel batteries at Pensacola Bay. Fort McRae silenced, and Fort Barracas greatly injured.

24th. Federal forces occupy Tybee Island, S. C.

26th. Second grand review of McClellan's forces, Washington.

27th. All commerce below St. Louis under Federal control.

28th. Great quantities of cotton burnt below Beaufort and Charleston. S. C.

December 3. Major Bowen's cavalry repulses the enemy at Salem, Missouri.

Reconnoisance of 125 of Parks' command. near Vienna, Va., are surprised by 300 rebels, but cut their way through, losing 45 killed, wounded, and missing.

4th. Colonel Taylor, with 80 men, in ambush, surprises and cuts to pieces 40 rebel cavalry, near Armadale, Va.

Memphis Avalanche demands raising the black flag.

7th. General John Pope assigned the Federal forces between the Missouri and Osage Rivers.

Captain Sweeny and guerrillas captured near Glasgow, Mo.

8th. General Stephens, commanding the Federal forces, occupies Port Royal Island and Beaufort, S. C.

9th. Federal gunboats bombard and destroy the enemy's position at Freestone Point.

General Cooper, with about 2,000 Texans and Indians has a severe battle at Rush River, in the Indian country, with about 2,500 loyal Indians, led by their Chief Opothelezholo. After much gallantry and great loss on both sides, the rebels withdrew fighting.

10th. Picket skirmish at dam No. 4, on the Potomac, in which a Federal company is entrapped and taken prisoners.

11th. Many Indians having been enticed into the Confederacy, are returning to Federal allegiance....It is announced that Kentucky has been received into the Confederacy during secret session.

12th. Over one-half the richest portion of Charleston burnt. The Confederacy appoints G. W. Johnson Provisional Gov. Ky.

13th. BATTLE OF ALLEGHANY SUMMIT.—The Federal troops under General R. H. Milroy, about 1,400 strong, assault the rebel stronghold at Alleghany Summit under Colonel E. Johnson, 2,000 strong, but is repulsed, owing to the want of artillery support, after a stubborn resistance from daylight to 3 P. M. Union loss, 21 killed, 107 wounded, and 10 missing; disunionists, 20 killed 96 wounded.

15th. Rebels fire Platte City, Mo., to "smoke out" the Federals.

16th. Kentucky Senators sworn into the Confederate Congress.

17th. The Thirty-second Indiana German regiment, encounter and repulse a strong rebel force under General Hindman at Mumfordsville, Ky., killing 33, and wounding 50.

18th. Colonel Jeff. C. Davis, with a division of General Pope's forces captures 1,300 prisoners at Milford, Mo., having 2 killed and 8 wounded.

Rebel camps taken on Edisto Island and Rockville, S. C.

19th. Colonel Geary's Twenty-eighth defeats a rebel battery after thirty minutes engagement, near Point of Rocks, killing and wounding 18......Ripley, Virginia, plundered by rebels.

20th. Stone fleet sunk on Charleston bar yesterday and to-day.

BATTLE OF GAINESVILLE, Va.—A Union foraging party under Brig.-Gen. Ord, of about 4,500, have a severe contest with about 2,500 rebels under Gen. Stewart, of near two hours, when the enemy retreat, with 70 killed, 143 wounded, 44 missing, and a large quantity of munitions of war left on the field. Union loss, 7 killed, 61 wounded, and 2 missing.

21st. Southern papers rejoice at the prospect of war between England and the United States.

22d. General Halleck orders any one convicted of bridge burning to be shot.

23d. Forty-seven Unionists defeat 118 rebels, wounding 16, in an engagement in Perry county, Kentucky.

24th. Unionists under General Stevens occupy Bluffton, S. C.

General Pope's cavalry destroy the foundry, ferry-boats, etc., at Lexington Mo., capturing 3 officers and 4 men.

26th. Rebels defeated in a skirmish at Columbia, Ky.

27th. Intelligence received that the Federal troops under Gen.

Canby, in New Mexico, have retaken Forts Craig and Stanton and, *en route* to retake Fort Fillmore.

Enemy in front of Washington announced as having gone into winter-quarters.

28th. General Prentiss with 450 troops, searching up bridge burners and rebel camps, in Northern Missouri, comes in contact with Colonel Dorsey's force of 900 at Mt. Zion Church, Boone county, defeating them with a loss of 150 killed and wounded, and 20 prisoners. Union loss, 3 killed and 11 wounded, with 95 horses and 105 guns.

Colonel Jackson's Kentucky cavalry in scouting comes in con-contact with 700 of Forrest's rebel cavalry, near South Carrolton, Ky. After a gallant hand to hand contest, the Federals fled, with a loss of 1 killed, 7 wounded and 4 prisoners. The rebel loss, including Col. Merriweather, 30 in all. Mason and Slidell given up.

29th. Jeff. Thompson's men pillage Commerce, Missouri.

30th. "First regular cartel passed between the Federal and Confederate authorities."

The steamer "Mt. Vernon" destroys the enemy's light vessel and local battery at Wilmington, N. C.

31st. Commodore M. Smith, with three national gunboats takes Biloxi, Mississippi.

1862.

January 1st. Battle on Port Royal Island, Federal troops victorious.... Mason and Slidell embark for Europe.

2d. Skirmish near Port Royal Ferry, S. C.

"Ella Warley" runs the blockade into Charleston with valuable cargo and dispatches for the Confederate Government.

3d. Two hundred and forty exchanged prisoners arrive at Fortress Monroe.... Big Bethel occupied.

4th. Gen. Jackson defeats a loyal force 1,000 strong, at Bath, Virginia...... The Federals capture and destroy $80,000 worth of supplies for the enemy at Huntsville, Va.

6th. Major-General G. B. Crittenden issues a proclamation calling on Kentuckians to enlist in behalf of their State and the Confederate cause.

7th. Enemy defeated at Blue Gap, Virginia...... Major Bowers defeats H. Marshall's rebel brigade near Painsville, Kentucky.

8th. Captain Latham routes a band of guerrillas in Randolph county, Virginia.

9th Colonel Harry Anisanel defeats some bushwhackers who had plundered Sutton, Virginia.... Defeat of 1,000 rebels after an hour's battle in Randolph county Mo., their plunder captured, and 30 killed, wounded and taken prisoners.

11th. To prevent shooting of pickets, General Grant orders all the inhabitants within six miles of Bird's Point, Mo., to be brought into camp and guarded.

Burnside's expedition from Fortress Monroe sails.

Colonel Garfield occupies Prestonburg, Kentucky.

13th. Secretary Cameron resigns; E. M. Stanton succeeds him.

17th. Burnside's expedition arrives off Hatteras, N. C.

19th. BATTLE OF MILL SPRING, Ky., begins at 5½ o'clock A. M., and continues till late in the afternoon. The rebel Generals Crittenden and Zollicoffer, with 8,000 men, advance and engage the forces commanded by General Thomas, 3,000 strong, but are defeated and driven from the field, leaving General Zollicoffer among the slain. Union loss, 39 killed, and 207 wounded; Rebel loss, 192 killed, 62 wounded, and 150 prisoners, 21 cannon, 600 muskets, over 1,200 horses and mules, 100 four-horse wagons, captured.

This is the first of a series of brilliant victories in the West, and secures Eastern Kentucky.

27th. Bishop E. Ames and Hon. Henry Fish, appointed Commissioners to visit Union prisoners in the South, to relieve their necessities and promote their comfort.

31st. Congress authorizes President Lincoln to take in military possession all railroads and telegraph lines in the United States.

February 6th. BATTLE OF FORT HENRY, Tenn.—The bombardment commences at 12½ o'clock, at a range of one mile, the Fort 2,600 strong. The fierce conflict continues for nearly an hour, when she surrenders to flag officer Foot. Gen. Grant's land forces arrives about an hour afterwards. Twenty guns, 17 mortars, and a vast amount of stores, etc., together with 70 prisoners, (the main body having fled), including General Tilghman, the commanding officer, fall in Federal hands. Union loss, 39 killed, wounded 23; rebel loss, 5 killed, 10 wounded.

8th. BATTLE OF ROANOKE ISLAND, N. C., commenced yesterday, terminating late this afternoon in favor of the loyal forces. Burnside during the night and morning landed about 5,000 troops—in all about 14,000. Several of the strong rebel works under Gen. Wise, 2,700 strong, were carried at the point of the bayonet. Six forts, mounting 42 guns, 3,000 stand of small arms, about 3,000 prisoners, with immense military stores, pass into Federal hands. Union loss, 50 killed, 222 wounded; the enemy have 23 killed, 58 wounded, 2,527 prisoners. Commodore Goldsborough's fleet of 31 gunboats acts in conjunction with Burnside's forces. The possession of this Island unlocks Albemarl and Currituck Sounds, and eight rivers, and first awakens censure against the rebel Government.

10th. Marshal law declared in Kansas. The Federal fleet returns from Florence, Alabama, having captured and destroyed several vessels and a vast amount of rebel stores. Elizabeth City Va., surrenders to Burnside's forces.

Commander Rowan engages the enemy's fleet this morning off Cobb's Point, N. C. silencing two land batteries. The enemy destroy five of their vessels, abandons two, and one is captured.

12th. General Curtis captures a large amount of stores from Price's army.... Colonel Reggin's forces return to Fort Henry with $75,000 worth of contraband goods, captured at Paris, Tenn.... The attack on FORT DONELSON, near 15,000 strong, commences ; the rebel pickets are driven in.

13th. The army before Fort Donelson remains quiet, awaiting reinforcements from Cairo...Springfield, Mo., occupied by loyal troops....Earl Russel declares his approval of the stone blockade in Charleston harbor, in the British House of Lords.

14th At 3 o'clock P. M. the gunboats resume attack on Fort Donelson, lasting one and a half hours. Gradually the rebel batteries cease firing, when two of the boats being disabled, Com. Foote orders the fleet to fall below.

Political prisoners to be released on taking an oath not to aid the rebellion or injure the United States Government.

General Lander reports the capture of many prisoners and large stores near Blooming Gap, Va.

Hon. Mr. Fish and Bishop Ames are in Washington, having been refused admittance within the rebel lines, but negotiated for the exchange of prisoners.

15th. Early this morning the enemy attack the Federal right, in front of Donelson ; for several hours the Union line wavers and is driven some distance, but reinforced, the rebels are driven upon their intrenchments. At 3 P. M. General Grant orders an assault upon the enemies rifle-pits, half a mile from the fort. These are carried by General Smith in the face of a terrible fire. Now General Wallace moves upon the rebel rifle-pits at the center and right ; after stubborn resistance drives the enemy within his works. The day closes with Grant, 30,000 strong, in possession of the outer fortifications.

16th. The white flag is seen on the ramparts of Fort Donelson in token of surrender. General Buckner surrenders to Grant with a loss of 10,000 men. 20,000 stand of arms, with vast quantities of ammunition, stores, etc. Generals Floyd and Pillow, with some 5,000 men escaped during the night. This victory secures West Tennessee, and the heaviest stroke yet to the enemy, and the largest number of prisoners ever taken in battle on this continent. Rebel loss, killed 231, wounded 1,007 ; Federal loss, 446 killed, 1,735 wounded, 150 prisoners.

17th. Two rebel regiments unaware of the surrender, march into Fort Donelson and are captured.... Great rejoicing in the North over recent victories.... BATTLE OF SUGAR CREEK, Ark.

18th. The notorious Quantrell and Parker routed at Independence, Mo... The rebel Congress permanently organized at Richmond Va.

20th. Skirmish at Occoquan, Va.

Burnside's fleet burns Winton, N. C.

21st. BATTLE OF FORT CRAIG, N. M., lasts all day, when the rebels under Col. Steele, nearly 2,000 strong, drive Col. Canby with 1,500 men, into the fort with a loss of 62 killed, and 140 wounded. Rebel killed and wounded, 120.

22d. Washington's birth day celebrated in the North....Martial law declared in West Tenn....Inauguration of Davis and Stevens.

23d. General Buel occupies Gallatin, Tenn...Fayetteville, Ark., captured by General Curtis...The rebels evacuate Nashville, Tenn.

March 2d. General Lander dies..Dupont's fleet takes Brunswick, Georgia.

3d. Union troops occupy Columbus, Kentucky.

General Banks occupies Martinsburg.

A battle of two hours between General Pope's forces and the rebels near New Madrid, Mo. Pope retreats.

Fernandina, Fla., captured by the land and naval forces of Gen. Wright and Com. Dupont.

5th. General Beauregard assumes command of the Mississippi army....Bunker Hill, Va., occupied by the Federal forces.

6th. BATTLE OF PEA RIDGE, Ark., commences by an attack from the rebels 35,000 on the right wing of the Union army, pressing Sigel's rear guard to their junction with the main army on Sugar Creek. At 4 P. M. the Federals reinforced, the rebels cease.

7th. The battle resumed by an attack on General Curtis with 20,000 men, and becomes general by 9 o'clock, raging all day with heavy losses; General McCullough, the rebel commander, among the slain.

8th. The Battle of Pea Ridge renewed at sunrise with the batteries of the centre and right of General Curtis' forces; The whole rebel line responds with great determination; the left wing and center are thrown forward, the left succeeds in turning the right of the enemy; this followed by a charge of the whole line results in the complete route of the enemy. Federal loss, killed 212, wounded 926, missing 174; enemy's loss, 1,100 killed, wounded 2,500, missing 1,600.

General Beauregard urges the planters to send in their bells to be cast into cannon for the defense of their plantations.

NAVAL BATTLE OF HAMPTON ROADS, Va.—The enemy's ironclad, "Merrimac," under Flag Officer Buchanan, attacks the U. S. frigates "Cumberland" and "Congress" under Flag Officer Marston. The fire from the "Cumberland" proves harmless on such an enemy; a stroke from the ram lays her sides open; she immediately sinks, carrying down nearly 100 heroes. The whole afair occupies fifteen minutes. The ram then turns upon the "Congress," which after an inefficient resistance surrenders, and is burnt. The Minnesota, in her flight from the ram, ran aground; the "St. Lawrence" in aid of the "Minnesota," also grounded, and is damaged by a shot. Night closes the scene.

9th. The Federal ironclad "Monitor," Lieutenant J. L. Worden, arrived during the night in aid of the Minnesota. The two ironclad rams engage each other for four hours, when the "Merrimac," with apparent injury, steamed away. The "Monitor" unhurt. The loss in killed, wounded and missing, 261. *Here dates a new era in the naval history of the world;* wooden vessels superceded by ironclads. The "Merrimac" the first ironclad vessel ever brought into action. Rebel loss, 7 killed, 17 wounded....Federals occupy Point Pleasant, Mo ...Skirmish at Burk's Station, Va.... Cockpit Point batteries captured

10th. Skirmish in Lafayette county, Mo....Skirmish near Jackson, East Tenn....Federal forces occupy Centreville, Va.

11th. McClellan occupies Manasses....Jeff. Davis suspends from command Generals Floyd and Pillow for misconduct at Fort Donelson....San Augustine, Fla., surrenders to Dupont and raises the United States flag.

12th. Forts in New York harbor garrisoned.... Winchester, Va., occupied by Federal troops....Skirmish at Paris, Tenn...... Federal troops occupy Berrysville, Va...... Fighting at Lebanon, Mo. Jacksonville, Fla., occupied by Federal troops....General Campbell taken prisoner.

13th. Skirmishes at Newport News and Winchester, Va. Gen. Halleck assumes command of the Mississippi Department.

BATTLE OF NEW MADRID, Mo.—General Pope brought his heavy siege guns and field pieces to bear on the rebel works this morning. The enemy responds with both their land and naval pieces. At nightfall the fort was closely invested by Federal troops, 12,000 strong; fearing an assault in the morning, the rebels, 9,000 strong, under Colonel Cowen, evacuated under cover of a heavy storm during the night.

14th. The fort, with its immense stores, valued at $1,000,000, together with nearly 9,000 infantry besides artillery, and 8 gun boats, under Com. Hollins, fall into Federal possession. Rebel killed, over 100. Federal loss, 61 killed and wounded.

BATTLE OF NEWBERN, N. C.—The rebels, commanded by General Branch, 10,000 strong, intrenched, with 21 guns and a large quantity of field artillery; the Federal forces under Burnside, 8,000 strong, sweep battery after battery until the last, when the enemy flee in the direction of Goldsboro. Federal loss, 91 killed, 466 wounded; enemy's loss, 100 killed, 200 wounded, and 200 missing, 46 siege guns, 3 batteries, 3,000 stand of small arms, military stores, etc.

16th. Bombardment of Island No. 10 commences....Skirmish at Pittsburgh Landing....Fight at Salem, Ark. Federal forces 250 strong, defeat 1,000 rebels. Federal loss, 25 killed and wounded; rebel loss, 100 killed and wounded.

18th. Bombardment continues.... General Pope, at New Madrid, permitted a rebel gunboat to steam within 50 yards of a masked battery, he then sunk her; making in all five steamers between his batteries unable to escape.

20th. Union meeting at Jacksonville, Fla.

21st. Dupont captures San Augustine.

23d. BATTLE OF WINCHESTER, Va.—The enemy, 10,000 strong, under General Jackson, attacks General Shields, with 7,000 men. The engagement continues from sunrise till noon, when a charge drives the enemy half a mile, but rallying, drives the Federal troops back. Both parties fight with desperation; the left flank of the enemy being turned, at 3 P. M., seized with a panic, fled. Union loss, 103, killed, wounded 441, missing 24; rebel loss, 350 killed, 1,000 wounded, 200 missing.

25th. Burnside takes Wilmington, N. C.

26th. Two hundred of Quantrell's men repulsed at Warrensburg, Mo....Skirmish at Hermanville, Mo....Skirmish at McMinville, Tennessee.

28th. Skirmish at Apache Canon, N. M., Federals 1,300 strong, rebels 2,000 strong. The enemy lost their entire train, with near 150 killed, 200 wounded, and 93 prisoners; Federal loss, 20 killed, 54 wounded, and 35 prisoners....Parker's guerrillas defeated near Warrensburg, Mo.

April 1st. Skirmish at Putnam's Ferry, Ark.; also at Woodstock, Va....Federal troops occupy Warrenton, Va.

3d. United States Senate abolishes slavery in the District of Columbia....Apalachacola, Florida, surrenders to Federal forces without resistance.

6th BATTLE OF SHILOH.—Generals Beauregard and Johnson, with a force 45,000 strong, engage the Federal forces under Generals Grant and Buel, 65,000 strong, at Pittsburgh Landing, Tennessee. The battle rages with fearful carnage all day; Grant's forces are pressed back to the river, with the loss of General Prentiss and 2,500 prisoners, 36 pieces of artillery, etc. The army is saved from disaster by the timely aid of the gunboats. General A. S. Johnson is killed, the Confederate military genius of the West. Buel's advance arrives at night, from Nashville, and crosses to Grant's relief.

7th. Early this morning the engagement becomes general, but Buel's fresh troops turn the tide of battle in favor of the Federal army. General Sherman's division pursues the retreating enemy. Union loss, 1,735 killed, including Brigadier-General Wallace, 7,882 wounded, and 3,956 prisoners and missing. Rebel loss, 1,728 killed, 8,012 wounded, 957 missing.

ISLAND No. 10, after a bombardment of 23 days, surrenders the garrison to Com. Foote, with 12,000 men, (part of the garrison escaped to the main land), 560 prisoners, including 17 officers, and nearly $250,000 worth of property.

8th. Com. Foote captures the retreating army at Tiptonville. Thus in the aggregate, 17 killed and 6,300 prisoners, 233 officers, 5,000 stand of arms, 2,000 horses and mules, 1,000 wagons, and $40,000 worth of provisions, fall into Federal hands....Rebels under McCall 7,000 strong....General Milroy occupies Monterey, Va.

9th. Great rejoicing over recent Union victories.........Federal troops defeated in a skirmish at Whitemarsh Island, Ga.

10th. President Lincoln, in view of recent victories, recommends the people to render thanks to Almighty God on the next Lord's day.

11th. SURRENDER OF FORT PULASKI, Ga.—On yesterday the garrison refused to surrender; at once the siege commenced, and operations were brisk during the day. At night the dismounted guns were brought to their places, and at early dawn a heavy fire is brought to bear on the Fort, which exposes her magazine through an opening in the wall. This terrifies the rebel garrison under Colonel Olmstead. At 2½ P. M. after a stubborn resistance, surrenderes to General Hunter, consisting of 385 prisoners, 47 guns, 7,000 shell and shot, 40,000 pounds of powder. Federal loss, 1 killed, and 1 wounded; enemy's loss, 3 wounded....Skirmish near Yorktown, Va....General Mitchell surprises Huntsville, Ala., stopping two trains for the east, capturing 17 locomotives, 150 cars, and 170 prisoners.

12th. In all, 58 vessels have run the blockade....The 19th South Carolina regiment refuses to leave the State....Federal troops capture 2,000 prisoners, 5 locomotives, etc., at Stevenson.....Commodore Foote's fleet sails for Fort Pillow, Tenn.

13th. Large rebel mail captured....Naval skirmish at Needham.

15th. General Canby defeats the enemy at Peralto, Texas. Federal loss, 25 killed and wounded....Skirmishing in front of Yorktown....Enemy driven from their works at Gloucester.

16th. Slavery abolished in District of Columbia....Rebels defeated at Savannah, Tenn, 5 killed, 65 wounded....Federal troops surprised at Wilmington, N. C., but rallied, when the enemy fell back to their batteries....61 of Ashley's men captured and carried into Woodstock, Va....Skirmish at Lee's Mills, Va. Federal loss, 35 killed, 120 wounded, 9 missing; enemy's loss, killed and wounded, 100.

18th. Fredericksburg surrenders to General Augur.

BOMBARDMENT OF FORTS JACKSON AND ST. PHILLIP commences by Farragut's fleet below New Orleans, and Butler with 8,000 land forces.

24th. Commodore Farragut runs the gauntlet past Forts Jackson and St. Phillip with but little damage, and engages the enemy's fleet in a terrible battle; 13 rebel gunboats and three transports destroyed; one Federal boat sunk, fighting to the last. The fleet anchors 20 miles below New Orleans; enemy's loss, 185 killed, 197 wounded, and 400 prisoners; Federal loss, 86 killed, and 119 wounded. Rebel land forces 10,000 strong.

25th. FORT MACON (N. C.) BOMBARDED.—The land batteries in connection with the fleet engage the fort all day.

26th. The fort surrenderes at 10 o'clock A. M. to the combined forces of Burnside and Lockwood (one brigade.) Federal loss, 1 killed, 11 wounded; enemy, under Col. White, 470 strong, killed 7, wounded 18.... President Lincoln goes on board the "Gassendi," a French man-of-war, and receives the same honors as the Emperor of France—the first President to visit a foreign man-of-war.

Skirmish at Neosho, Missouri.

28th. Forts Jackson and St. Phillip being surrounded and cut off, surrender to Com. Porter.... New Orleans, the largest exporting city in the world, surrenders to Com. Farragut.... Skirmish at Monterey, Tenn.

30th. BATTLE AT BRIDGPORT, Ala.—Rebel loss, 72 killed, 350 prisoners.

May 2d. The port of New Orleans opened to commerce.

5th. BATTLE OF WILLIAMSBURG, Va.—McClellan's advance engages the enemy under Gen. Johnson, about 25,000 strong. The battle rages all day; Hancock, towards night, turns the rebel left, when they retreat under cover of night. Federal loss, 456 killed, 1,400 wounded, and 372 missing; rebel loss, 700 killed, 1,000 wounded, and 300 prisoners.

7th. BATTLE OF WEST POINT, Va.—The enemy attack Gen. Franklin's division, but are repulsed after a hard battle of 7½ hours, with a loss of 1,000 killed and wounded; Federal killed not reported, wounded about 300, prisoners 500....General McClellan's advance within 33 miles of Richmond.

8th. Generals Milroy and Schenck, with nine regiments of Federal troops, engage 14,000 rebel troops under Jackson, at McDowell, Va., The battle lasts from 6 to 9 P. M., when the United States forces retire to Franklin. Federal loss, 30 killed, 216 wounded; rebel loss unknown.

9th. The enemy evacuate Pensacola, Fla..... Fight at Slater's Mills, Va...... General McClellan thanked by the United States House of Representatives.

BATTLE OF FARMINGTON, Miss.—General Bragg's forces are held in check five hours, when reinforced, the Federal forces under Pope, 3,500 strong, retreat. Union loss, 21 killed, 140 wounded

Burnside destroys $50,000 worth of provisions designed for the rebels.

10th. Union meeting in Shepardsville, N. C.... Surrender of Norfolk.... Naval engagement on the Mississippi; the Federal fleet victorious.... General Butler seizes $800,000 at the Consulate of the Netherlands in New Orleans.... Rebels burn Gosport Navy Yard.

11th. The rebel "Merrimac" blown up by her commander..... 140 of Morgan's cavalry captured at Cave City, Ky.... Canary Island, Va., occupied by Union forces.

12th. General McClellan, reconnoitreing near the rebel lines barely escapes capture.

13th. General Butler suppresses the New Orleans Crescent. Suffolk, Va., occupied....Skirmish at Monterey, Tenn...Natchez surrenders to Com. Palmer....General Negley occupies Rodgersville, Ala....General Butler suppresses the observance of a "fast day," as appointed by "*one* JEFFERSON DAVIS."

14th. The steamer "Alice," captured near Williamstown, having on board the church bells of Plymouth, N. C., to be cast into rebel field pieces....Skirmish at Trenton Bridge, N. C.

16th. Butler suppresses the New Orleans Bee, and takes military possession of the Delta office....Rebel conscription Act goes into effect.

18th. Surrender of Vicksburg demanded....Skirmish at Princeton, Va....150 Union troops defeat 600 rebels at Searcy, Ark.

19th. General Stoneman's cavalry within 14 miles of Richmond. ....General Hunter's Emancipation Proclamation repudiated by President Lincoln.....The rebels at City Point, Va., fire on a flag of truce, one man only escapes....The Mayor of New Orleans arrested and sent to Fort Jackson.

21st. BATTLE OF PHILLIPS' CREEK, Miss.—The rebels repulsed, leaving a great amount of provisions and stores in the hands of General Davis....Skirmish near Corinth....Artillery fighting at Fort Pillow.

22d. Union meeting at Portsmouth, Va....McClellan croses the Chickahominy.

23d. Ewel, with a heavy force, drives Col. Kenley from Front Royal, Va.; Union loss heavy......Capt. Tilford, with 40 men, engages 200 rebels for three hours, when he retreats to Fort Craig, N. M., 3 wounded.

BATTLE OF LEWISBURG, Va.—General Heath, commanding 3,000 rebels, attacks two regiments under Col. Cook, one hours' battle puts the rebels to flight, leaving 38 dead, and 66 wounded on the field, 100 prisoners, 300 stand of arms taken; Union loss, 10 killed, 40 wounded.

24th. General Stoneman, the advance of the Army of the Potomac, within five miles of Richmond....Skirmish at Cold Harbor. ....The expense of the war since April 1st, has averaged $1,000,000 per day....General Banks reaches Winchester, on his retreat from Strasburg....United States Government calls for more troops.

25th. BATTLE OF WINCHESTER, Va.—Gen. Banks with 5,000 men resolves to check the enemies' advance, under Stonewall Jackson, with about 18,000 rebels, from an advantagious position he engages the enemy for 5 hours inflicting severe loss. He then continues his retreat across the Potomac. Union killed 38, wounded 155, missing 711. Rebels no report.

27th....Fitz-John Porter defeats the enemy at Hanover Court House; 100 killed, and 500 prisoners......Norfolk Day-Book suppressed....Sigel called to Washington....Bombardment of Fort Pillow resumed.

29th. The rebels attack General Casey's pickets and drive them back near the "Seven Pines," but reinforced, regain their former

position.....Beauregard evacuates Corinth.....The New Orleans Bee resumes publication, having made explanations to Gen. Butler.
30th. General Jackson repulsed in an attempt to dislodge the National troops at Harper's Ferry....Halleck occupies Corinth; his force about 100,000
31st. Union troops repulsed at Neosho, Mo....Skirmish near Washington, N. C....General Banks, reinforced, advances beyond Martinsburg.

BATTLE OF FAIR OAKS.—At 10 A. M., the main body of the enemy, under Joe Johnson, about 35,000 strong, taking advantage of a heavy storm, attacks the Union advance. Gen. Casey's division being overpowered, falls back; Couch's division rallies to their assistance, and checks their further advance. The battle is desperate. At 6 o'clock disaster is imminent, but Sedgwick marches into action and turns the tide of battle At night the rebels occupy the ground they won. General J. E. Johnson, the rebel commander, wounded; nearly everything belonging to Casey's division captured.

June 1st. The battle resumed at daylight, and rages all day. By a most daring and brilliant charge of the bayonet, the rebels lost their position and fled toward Richmond. Union loss, 890 killed, 3,627 wounded, 1,222 missing; enemy's loss, 2,800 killed, 3,897 wounded, 814 missing.

2d. General Hunter's forces, operating against Charleston, S. C. ....Skirmish at Washington, N. C....General Fremont defeats Jackson near Strasburg.

3d. General Hooker reconnoitreing within 4 miles of Richmond. ....Gen. R. E. Lee assumes command of the Army at Richmond.

4th. General Halleck reports General Pope being 30 miles south of Florence, Ala., with 40,000 men, having captured 10,000 prisoners, 15,000 stand of arms, and 9 locomotives....Skirmish at Jasper, Tenn.; rebels defeated....1,600 Union prisoners at Nashville paroled by the rebels because they were not able to provision them.

5th. Federal fleet arrives before Memphis.

6th. BATTLE OF MEMPHIS, Tenn.—Triumphant naval engagement near Memphis, under Flag Officer, C. H. Smith, in which the rebel fleet under Montgomery was almost annihilated, Union loss, one wounded; rebel loss, 80 killed and wounded....Memphis surrenders....McClellan's army crosses the Chickahominy......Fremont captures the enemy's camp at Harrisonburg, Va.

7th. Rebel batteries silenced at Chattanooga.

8th. BATTLE OF CROSS KEYES, Va.—General Fremont with about 20,000 men, engages General Jackson with 17,000, at 8½ A. M., and drives him out after a hard fought battle. Federal loss, 125 killed, 500 wounded and missing; rebel loss, about 600....The rebel Gen. Ashby killed.

9th. Jackson, in his retreat, defeats the advance of Gen. Shield's division, 3,000 strong, at PORT REPUBLIC, Va....A reconnoitreing party within three miles of Charleston.

10th. The enemy defeated on JAMES ISLAND, S. C., after a battle of two hours. Their loss, 17 killed, 30 wounded, 6 prisoners; Federal loss, 3 killed, 13 wounded....Fremont at Port Republic.

12th. Skirmish near village Creek, Ark.; enemy defeated, 28 killed and wounded; Union loss, 1 prisoner, 12 wounded... Skirmishing on the Chickahominy.

13th. United States flag raised at Grêtna, La., amid great rejoicing....Another skirmish on James Island; rebels defeated, with 19 killed, and 6 wounded; Federal loss, 3 killed, 19 wounded.

14th. Captain Atkinson, with 20 men, captures 6,200 pounds of powder at Sycamore Mills.

15th. Gen. Stuart makes a cavalry raid through the lines of the right wing of the U. S. army, and destroys two schooners on the Pamunkey, returning around the left wing enters Richmond to-day.....The Monitor at City Point.

16th. The Union forces, about 6,000 strong, repulsed in an attempt to dislodge the rebels in their intrenchments at Secessionville, on James Island.

20th. Gen. Sherman occupies Holly Springs, Miss....Daily skirmishing before Richmond....Lincoln approves the bill prohibiting slavery in the territories of the U. S.

25th. BATTLE OF OAK GROVE, VA.—Gen. Hooker's division of the Army of the Potomac, repulses the enemy after seven hours hard fighting. This is the first of the seven battles before Richmond. Union loss, 280 killed and wounded; rebel loss, about 500 in all. Gen. McClellan changes his base of operations to the James River. ....Union ram fleet arrives at Vicksburg and communicates with Farragut.

26th. Enemy's batteries at Vicksburg shelled for 3 hours by Porter's mortar fleet.*...BATTLE OF MECHANICSVILLE.—Gen. Lee, with about 20,000 men, attacks Gen. McCall, about 14,000 strong, at noon. This was one of the hardest fought, and most terrific battles of the campaign. The enemy finally repulsed. Rebels loss in all, about 450; Union loss, 80 killed, about 150 wounded.

27th. BATTLE OF GAINS' MILLS.—The Union troops 35,000, are attacked by 70,000 rebels attempting to break their lines in various places, by concentrating at these points, but are checked in every instance, until the Union left wing gives way, when they retreat, but reinforced, the enemy's advance is checked The enemy holds the field. Union loss, 7,500; rebel loss, about two-thirds as much.....McClellan evacuates White House, Va....Severe skirmish at Village Creek, Ark.

29th. BATTLE OF PEACH ORCHARD, VA.—The Union troops being pressed by the rebels, hold their fire for close range, when it is delivered with such effect for one-half an hour, that it seems "like the continuous echo of a single report." Gen. Burns' brigade endures the main heat of the battle. Union loss, 150; rebels, 1,500. This was a decisive victory, the battle lasting 4 hours—a small force against a large one....Bombardment of Vicksburg continues.

29th. BATTLE OF SAVAGES STATION, Va.—The strength of the forces are not reporteed. McClellan's forces fall back from Peach Orchard and fight this battle in the afternoon, the enemy reinforced with men and batteries; after an obstinate contest, late in the evening, the enemy are repulsed. Union loss, about 800. Rebel loss, unknown.

30th. BATTLE OF WHITE OAK SWAMP.—Continues nearly all day, as the Union troops approach James River. The gunboats check the advance of the enemy by pouring a galling fire into their ranks. Night closes the scene, but not till the enemy is defeated. McClellan's forces nearly 90,000, lose 4,000; Lee's forces exceed the Unionists, loss, over 4,000.

July 1st. BATTLE OF MALVERN HILL.—The Union forces under McClellan, 85,000 strong, took a position on Malvern Hill, under cover of the gunboats, and are attacked by the combined forces of Lee, but are repulsed at all points; with the fall of night the battle ceases. Union loss, about 1,000; rebel loss, 3,000. This closes the seven days struggle.... BATTLE OF BOONEVILLE, MISS.—Col. Sheridan defeats 4,700 rebels in 4 hours hard fighting; they left 65 dead on the field. Unionists, 41 killed, wounded and missing.... The President calls for 300,000 troops.

2d. The rebel army paralyzed and Richmond at the mercy of McClellan, but we have the spectacle of both armies in full retreat. McClellan reaches Harrisons Landing on James' River.

3d. The news of the retreat of the Army of the Potomac creates great excitement in the North.... City Point, Virginia, destroyed.

4th. The National Anniversary enthusiastically celebrated.

6th. BATTLE OF GRAND PRAIRIE, ARK.—200 loyal troops against 440 rebel cavalry; the rebels defeated with a loss of 84 killed, wounded and missing.

7th. BATTLE OF CACHE, ARK.—Between 200 rebels and 400 loyal troops, reinforced near the termination of the engagement by 200 cavalry, commanded by C. E. Hovey. The rebels defeated with a loss of 200 killed, besides a great number wounded and prisoners; Union loss, 7 killed, 85 wounded.

8th. President Lincoln reviews the National troops at Harrison's Landing.... Burnside's army forms a junction with McClellan's.

9th. Morgan's guerillas, 1,500 strong, defeat 250 loyal troops under Major Jordan, with a loss of 4 killed.... Public meetings held in England to induce the Government to mediate in the war, and if necessary, acknowledge the independence of the Southern Confederacy.

11th. Gen. Halleck appointed General-in-Chief of the Armies of the United States.... Skirmish at Pleasant Hill, Mo. Rebels defeated, having 6 killed and 5 wounded.... Skirmish at Williamsburg, Va. Rebels routed with a loss of 3 killed and 7 prisoners. .... Rebel General Ruggles forbids the people of St. Tammany Parish to exchange their manufactures for food with the people of New Orleans.

12th. Gen. John Morgan defeats the Union troops at Lebanon, Ky.... Gen. Smith thanks his troops for their gallant defense of Vicksburg against the Union troops.... Skirmish at Culpepper, Va.... About 200 Unionists of North Alabama join the Union troops at Decatur, Ala.

13th. Murfreesboro, Tennessee, taken by the rebel Forrest, with the whole garrison, including Gens. Crittenden and Duffield, destroying 20,000 worth of property; Union loss, 33 killed, 100 wounded, over 800 missing; rebel loss, killed 50, wounded 100.

15th. Gen. Twiggs dies at Augusta, Ga.... Major Miller, with 600 cavalry, defeats a rebel force 1,600 strong, near Fayetteville, Arkansas, with great loss.... Gen. Blunt defeats the enemy in the Indian Territory; they lost 200 men.

17th. Morgan captures Cynthiana, Ky.... Cincinnati greatly excited, apprehending an attack from Morgan.

21st. The rebels celebrate the anniversary of the battle of Manassas.

22d. The Union ram "Queen of the West" defeated by the rebel ram "Arkansas."... For 12 days the rebel Col. Morgan has been in receipt of all telegraphic messages from head-quarters in Louisville.

28th. The office of the Herald at St. Stevens, New Brunswick, annihilated by a mob, for advocating the Union cause.... Skirmish at Moore's Mills, Mo.

29th. The citizens drive off the guerrillas at Mt. Sterling, Kentucky, killing 75 men..... The rebels routed at Bollinger's Mills, Mo.... Guerrillas capture Russville, Ky., after overpowering the home guards.... Skirmish at Brownsville, Tenn.

30th. The rebel Col. John Morgan reports having traveled 1,000 miles in 24 days, captured 17 towns, dispersed 1,500 home guards, and paroled near 1,000 regular troops, and lost but 90 men of the 1,200 with which he entered Ky.

August 1st. The Federals defeated at Newark, Mo.... Skirmishing along the Rapidan.

2d. Bell Boyd, the famous woman spy, arrested and sent to Washington.

3d. Gen. Burnside's army arrives at Acquia Creek····Gen. Halleck orders the evacuation of the Peninsula.

5th. BATTLE OF BATON ROUGE, LA.—The enemy, under Gens. Breckenridge and Ruggles, 6,000 strong, attack the Federals under Gen. Williams, 2,500 strong, with great determination, driving them from their position; but, rally and drive the enemy from the field, leaving their dead and wounded. Union loss, 60 killed, including Gen. Williams, 100 wounded and 29 missing; rebel loss, 400 killed, 600 wounded, 102 prisoners.... Gen. Hooker engages the rebels 2 hours at Malvern Hill, when the latter retreats.

6th. Enemy defeated at Montevallo, Mo.... The rebel ram "Arkansas" destroyed by the "Essex."

7th. Col. Canby defeats the rebel Gen. Sibley, near Fort Fillmore, New Mexico.

8th. Continued skirmishing in Mo.... Gen. Pope's pickets driven across the Rapidan by the advance of Lee's army from Richmond.
9th. BATTLE OF CEDAR MOUNTAIN.—Gen. Jackson, 20,000 strong, crosses the rapidan, and takes a strong position. Gen. Banks, with 7,000 men, advances and engages the enemy. At 6 o'clock, P. M. the battle is in full blast, and rages with great fury for 2 hours; the artillery, however, did not cease until near midnight. Banks, finding himself outnumbered, near 7 o'clock falls back to the support of Pope, who is near by. The enemy is now driven in confusion to his original position. This is a drawn battle. On the 11th, Jackson recrosses the Rapidan. Federal loss, killed 450, wounded 660, missing 290; enemy's loss, killed 223, wounded 1,060, missing 31.... Government orders the enrollment of the millitia in the Northern States.... Enemy repulsed with heavy loss at Farewell, Tenn.
10th. Admiral Farragut destroys Donaldsonville, La, for affording cover to the enemy to fire on the fleet.
11th. The Federals overpowered and defeated at Independence, Mo.... McClellan's army commences to evacuate the Peninsula. .... Skirmish at Cedar Mountain.... Guerrillas dispersed near Helena, Ark.... Guerrillas defeated by Col. Guitar, near Compton Ferry, Mo., with a loss of 100 killed and wounded, and 200 prisoners.... The property of John Slidell confiscated.
12th. Morgan captures Gallatin, Tenn.
13th. Gen. Hovey defeats Hindman at Clarendon, Mo.; many killed on both sides; enemy lost 700 prisoners.
14th. The rebel Gen. Breckenridge threatens to raise the black flag.
16th. Col. Corcoran and others arrive at Fortress Monroe, having been exchanged.... Major Foster, with 800 millitia, defeated by Coffee's guerrillas, with a loss of 60 killed.
17th. Aschbishop Hughes preaches a patriotic sermon at New York.
19th. More than 100 men, women and children massacred by the Sioux Indians at New Ulm, Minn. Skirmishing nearly every day.
21st. Federals defeated at Gallatin, Tenn., with 30 killed, 50 wounded, 75 prisoners.
22d. The rebels defeated in a series of skirmishes near Crab Orchard, Ky.... Stuart's cavalry dash into Catlett's Station, capturing Gen. Pope's papers.
25th. The rebel Col. Woodward with 75 men, defeated at Fort Donelson.
27th. Gen. Hooker's division of Pope's army, 9,000 strong, defeats the enemy 10,000 strong, under Ewell, at Kettle Run, with a loss of 300 killed and wounded, 1,000 prisoners, and their entire camp; Hooker's loss, nearly 300.
28th. Sigel and McDonald defeats the rebel Jackson, with great loss, at Centreville.

29th. *Battle of Groveton.*—The Federals under Pope engage the enemy under Jackson and Longstreet, and finally drive them from the field with a great loss.

Battle of Richmond, Ky.—Gen. Mason, 7,000 strong, with artillery, engages the enemy under Smith with 16,000 men, the whole line becoming one battle scene. After 1 hour's fight, the enemy is driven from the field.

30th. At 6 A. M., the Federals are driven back; the battle rages all day with varied success to our army, but the Federals are finally defeated with a loss of 200 killed, 700 wounded, and 2,000 prisoners; rebel loss, 50 killed and 500 wounded....A severe contest at *Bolivar, Tennessee,* of 2 hours; the Union troops being reinforced, the enemy withdraw with a large loss.

Second Battle of Bull Run.—Gen. Lee, with superior numbers, attackes the Union troops under Pope 40,000 strong, on the old field of Bull Run. The battle rages all day with fearful slaughter; the Federal left wing is finally pressed back a half mile, the right holding its position. After this engagement the army retreates to Centerville. Union loss, 800 killed, 4,000 wounded, 3,000 prisoners; Rebel loss, 700 killed, 3,000 wounded.

Sept. 1st. *Battle of Chantilly, Va.*—Lasts nearly an hour, commencing at sunset; the enemy is finally defeated at all points. Maj. Gen. Kearncy, and Brig. Gen. Stevens killed. This is the last of a series of battles fought by the Army of the Potomac in their retreat. The Federals lost about 1,300; rebels, not reported.

2d. McClellan placed in command of the defences of Washington....The enemy defeated with great loss at Morgansfield, Ky.... Orderly Sergeant Green, with about 300 men, engage and rout 1,400 rebels near Plymouth, N. C.

3d. Gen. Pope's army in the intrenchments of Washington. Pope asks to be relieved of his command.

6th. Gen. Lee occupies Frederick City, Md.

7th.. Great excitement in Pennsylvania on the advance of the enemy towards Hagarstown.

8th. The enemy defeated and lose nearly all their horses on the Mississippi, above New Orleans....Gov. Bradford calls into service the millitia of Maryland....Gen. Keyes repulses Stuart's cavalry at Edward's Ferry with the loss of 90 men.

10th. Union troops defeated at Fayette, Va....Natchez surrenders after a bombardment of 2 hours.

11th. The rebels carry off all the boots, shoes and clothing in Westminster, Md....The rebel Kirby Smith's forces 7 miles from Cincinnati.

12th. The engagement at Maryland Heights openes early and continues to 3 *P. M.,* when the forces retreats to Harper's Ferry.

14th. BATTLE OF SOUTH MOUNTAIN, Md.—Gen. McClellan, with 30,000 men, comes upon the enemy near Middletown, Md.... Franklin holds Burketsville Gap; Hooker and Reno carry the hights; the enemy desert the field together with their dead and wounded under cover of night. Union loss, 312 killed, 1,234 wounded, and 22 missing; rebels under Lee, 30,000 strong, loss 500 killed, 2,343 wounded, 1,500 prisoners.

15th. Rebel General Jackson captures Harper's Ferry; Union loss, 80 killed, (among these, Col. Miller,) 120 wounded, 10,500 surrender, 47 pieces of artillery, etc. Rebel loss unknown.

17th. BATTLE OF ANTIETAM, Md.—Gen. McClellan's forces, 87,164 strong; rebels under Lee, 97,000; the line of battle some 4 miles in extent. The action commenced by skirmishing under Hooker, yesterday. Renewed at 5 A. M. with dreadful slaughter, and alternate and varied success all day. At the fourth advance, the Federal forces hold the ground considered the key of position. Burnside, at 1 o'clock P. M. carries the stone bridge at the point of the bayonet; at 4 P. M. he and Franklin, holding the center, charges forward and held their position; the former carries the hills in his front in handsome style, but the enemy being strongly reinforced, Burnside is overpowered and forced back to his former position. Night closes the bloody scene, but victory to neither side. Preparations made to renew the battle in the morning, but during the night the enemy retreated. Federal loss, 2,010 killed, 9,416 wounded, 1,043 missing; total, 12,463. Enemy acknowledge a loss of from 14,000 to 15,000. Generals Richardson and Rodman mortally wounded. McClellan estimates their loss at 3,500 killed, 16,399 wounded, and about 2,660 prisoners; total, 22,559. No guns or colors lost by the Federal forces.

General Bragg after four days battle at Mumford, Ky., captures the Union forces, 4,000 strong, 4,000 stand of arms, stores, etc.

18th. Rebel General Bragg notifies Kentucky that the Army of the West has come to restore their liberties.

19th. BATTLE AT IUKA, Miss.—General Rosecrans commands the Federal forces, 20,000 strong, and General Price those of the enemy, 23,000 strong. The battle was severely contested for two hours, when darkness closes the scene. Price, during the night, retreats, leaving his captured guns, wounded, stores, etc. Price lost 385 killed, 692 wounded, and 561 prisoners; Union loss, 141 killed, 598 wounded, and 36 missing.

20th. Six skirmishes.

21st. San Francisco, Cal., contributes $100,000 to the Sanitary Commission.

22d. Rebels defeated with great loss at Ashby's Gap, Va.

President Lincoln gives notice of his intention to issue the EMANCIPATION PROCLAMATION on the 1st of January, 1863.

23d. Col. Sibley repulses 300 Indians in Minnesota, after two hours fighting; loss, 30 killed, and a great many wounded.... It is reported that the feeling was freely expressed in the Confederate House of Representatives of raising the black flag during the war.

30th. Continued skirmishing.

October 3. BATTLE OF CORINTH, Miss.—The armies of Price, Van Dorn, and Lovell, (28,000 men) combine in the action against the Federal forces under Rosecrans, (20,000 strong) at Corinth. The battle rages from early dawn till nightfall. The United States troops are driven from their position.

4th. The enemy renew the battle of Corinth at early dawn with great determination ; it terminates about noon in a hand-to-hand combat, in which the enemy are driven from the field. Federal loss, 315 killed, (including Gen. Hackelman,) 1,812 wounded, and 232 prisoners, and one missing ; enemy's loss, 1,423 killed, 5,692 wounded, 2,248 prisoners, (including 137 officers,) 3,300 stand of arms, 14 stand of colors, stores, etc. The enemy pursued 40 miles by the infantry, 60 by cavalry.

5th. The retreating enemy from Corinth, overtaken at HATCHIE RIVER by the forces of Generals Ord and Hurlburt. A battle of seven hours hard fighting throw the enemy into disorder, when they flee, leaving their dead and wounded, and 400 prisoners, and near 1,000 stand of arms. The Union loss, 500 killed and wounded. They capture at Nolan's ferry the personal effects and official documents of Gen. Longstreet.

6th. Col. Sibley, in Minnesota, has rescued from the Indians 107 whites and 162 half-breed Indians.

7th. BATTLE OF LAVERGNE, Tenn.—A force from Nashville assails the enemy's camp,. after an engagement of half an hour the rebels flee, with a loss of 80 killed and wounded ; Federal loss 14 killed and wounded.

8th. BATTLE OF CHAPLIN HILLS, Ky.—General McCook, 18,000 strong, attacked by the enemy under Bragg, 33,000 strong ; the contest is severe for several hours, when the enemy are driven across the river with severe loss. Federal loss, 820 killed, including Gens. Jackson and Terrell, 2,585 wounded, 650 prisoners. Rebel loss, killed, 1,300, wounded 3,000, prisoners 200. It is said this battle prevented Buel from capturing Bragg's troops.

9th. Skirmish of five hours near Lawrenceburg, Ky., resulting in the route of the enemy.

10th. *Stuart's Raid.*—General Stuart, with 1,800 cavalry and 4 pieces of artillery, captures Chambersburg, Pa.... Gov. Letcher, of Virginia, announces certain regulations for obtaining salt for the people.

12th. Stuart's cavalry returns with 1,000 horses, after doing damage to the amount of $150,000.

20th. Skirmishing each day.

22d. *Battle of Pocotaligo*, S. C.—Union loss, 43 killed, 25 wounded, 5 missing ; rebel loss not reported.

Federal forces under General Blunt engage the enemy, 5,000 strong, at *Maysville,* Ark. An hour's battle results in the comple route of the enemy, with a loss of 150 killed and wounded, together with their artillery, and part of their equippage ; Union loss, 5 killed and 9 wounded.

28th. Federal forces 1,000 strong, commanded by Gen. Herron, engage a superior force of rebels near Fayetteville, Ark. After an hour and a half the enemy flee from the field.

29th. 240 men of the First Kansas Colored Regiment, engage several hundred guerrillas at Dick's Ford, on the Osage. These troops are said to have executed their task with much courage, putting the enemy to flight.

30th. From 300 to 500 of Stewart's cavalry surprised near Petersburgh, Va. General Rosecrans succeeds General Buel.

November 2d. Skirmish at Philmont; enemy defeated.... Up to this date the rebel privateer "Alabama," has destroyed 19 vessels, and released one, and put two under bonds.

3d. The enemy defeated at Upperville by Gen. Pleasanton, after four hour's engagement, with a loss of 9 killed and several wounded. ....General Stahl forces the rebels out of Thoroughfare Gap, and occupies it..... Colonel Foster overtakes and defeats the foe in Webster county, Ky.; 3 killed, 2 wounded, 25 prisoners taken, and 40 horses.... General Porter's cavalry defeats the enemy at Snicker's Gap. Union loss, 5 killed, 16 wounded.

5th. General Burnside succeeds McClellan in the command of the Army of the Potomac.... The army divided into 3 corps, commanded by Major-Generals McCook, Thomas, and Crittenden.... Seven skirmishes to-day.

7th. 300 Indians sentenced to be hung, as perpetrators of the massacres in Minnesota.... Gen. Bragg's estate in Louisiana confiscated.

8th. Butler closes all the distilleries and breweries in his department......Rebels routed at Gaines' Cross Roads.

11th. 1,016 Federal, and 1,596 rebel officers, and 21,000 privates exchanged to-day...... Skirmishes in Tennessee and Kentucky.

14th. Army of the Potomac divided in three grand divisions, commanded by Generals Sumner, Franklin, and Hooker.

16th. President Lincoln commands the observance of the Sabbath in the Army and Navy.

27th. Gen. Washburn, with 1,925 men, leaves Helena, Ark., for a raid into Mississippi.

28th. Gen. Blunt defeats Marmaduke's rebel forces at Crane Hill, Ark.. They fight over 12 miles of ground.

29th. Gen. Stahl disperses the rebels at Snicker's Gap, killing 50 and capturing 40.

Dec. 1st. The noted Pittsburg battery recaptured from the enemy at Franklin, Va.

2d. Gen. Hovey, with a force of 20,000 men, occupies Grenada, Miss. The enemy before leaving, destroyed 15 locomotives, and 100 cars....Skirmishing each day.

7th. *Battle of Prairie Grove, Ark.*—Preceded by several days' skirmishing, commences this morning. The rebels in force attack Gen. Herron's 12,000, at the same time making a feint in front of Blunt. Gen. Blunt hearing the firing in the direction of Herron, who is coming to reinforce him, at once advances to the scene of action, arriving in time to prevent a flank movement on Herron's right wing. About 2 the entire line becomes engaged; the battle rages with fearful slaughter till night closes the scene. During the night, the rebels abandon the field with their dead and wounded. Union loss, killed, 167, wounded 798, and missing, 183; enemy's loss, killed 164, wounded 817, and 336 missing.

13th. *Battle of Fredericksburg.*—The city has been bombarded for 2 days; on yesterday afternoon, the pontoons being laid, Burnside's army crossed the river. This morning the rebel works are attacked. Hooker advances against the centre, while Franklin moves against the rebel right; charge succeeds charge, but fails to reduce the enemy's works. At midnight, each army occupies the same position as in the morning Union loss was, 1,512 killed, 9,105 wounded, and about 700 prisoners; enemy not reported.

15th. The Army of the Potomac still at Fredericksburg, the enemy holding their intrenchments.

16th. Burnside's army during the night and this morning, recrossed the river, before the enemy gained a knowledge of the movement. There was neither loss of life or property.

19th. Gen. Naglee captures 1,800 head of cattle in Gloucester county, Va.

20th. Hollow Springs, Miss., captured by Van Dorn's cavalry, with 1,500 prisoners, who are paroled; destroys $6,000,000 of property.

25th. Col. Morgan defeats the rebel Van Dorn at Davis' Mills, Miss., after a desperate battle of 3½ hours.... Col. Gray with 200 men, defeats 400 of Morgan's cavalry near Hardyville, Ky.

27th. Four severe skirmishes to-day. The outworks at *Vicksburg* attacked by Gen. Sherman, while the gunboats engage the Haines' Bluff batteries. The rebels driven from their works.

28th. To-day's battle results in the capture of the first and second lines; the contest is severe.... Gens. Herron and Blunt capture Van Buren, Ark.... Col. Morgan, with a force of 2,800 men, captures the Union garrison at Elizabethtown, Ky., after a severe contest of an hour.

29th. The Union forces carry the main battery and rifle pits in the rear of Vicksburg, but the rebels being reinforced, and massing all on Sherman, force him back to the outer works; the fighting in many instances is hand to hand. The artillery fire is terrible and lasts 3 hours. Sherman lost in killed, 191, wounded, 982, missing, 756; enemy's loss not reported.

30th. Morgan defeated at New Haven, Ky.

History of the Great Rebellion. 43

31st. *Battle of Murfreesboro, Tenn.* — Gen. Rosecrans, with 43,000 men, moves against the rebel army 68,000 strong, under Johnson, near Stewart's Creek, driving them into their works on Stone River, 3 miles from Murfreesboro. Harker's brigade moves across the river, supposing the enemy are retreating, where they encounter the fire of a regiment in ambush. Harker, holding his fire until within short distance, fires and charges, when the enemy are driven back upon the main body; Harker then withdraws to the main army. Yesterday there was considerable fighting and manœuvering for position, which was to the advantage of the Union forces. At daylight this morning Hardee moves cautiously in heavy force against McCook, who commands the right wing, and after an hour of desperate fighting the right wing is driven back over 3 miles, loosing 20 pieces of artillery. This artful stroke of the enemy foils the original design of the battle. The right wing being reinforced, and a new line formed, the artillery massed in the centre, belches forth terrible destruction on the advancing foe; being checked, a furious charge brakes their lines, when they flee from a bloody field of ten hours' battle.

1863.

Jan. 1st. Heavy skirmishing, but no general engagement along Gen. Rosecrans' line.

President Lincoln issues the Emancipation Proclamation, by which the fetters fall from Five and a half Millions of Slaves.

BATTLE OF GALVESTON, TEXAS.—Gen. Magruder, with 5,000 men and 5 steamers, attacks Col. Burrill with about 500 men, and 2 or 3 steamers. The engagement lasts 4 hours, the rebels being several times driven back, but at last the Unionists surrender to overpowering numbers. The Unionists lost the Harriet Lane and blew up the Westfield, 30,000 rifle cartridges, 5,000 picks and shovels.

The 12th Kentucky, under Col. Hoskins, attacks and defeats Morgan's forces near Lebanon, Ky., taking 60 prisoners, killing and wounding a number.

2d. BATTLE OF MURFREESBORO resumed.—Enemy masses his forces against the Union left, and advances at 3 o'clock P. M., in three heavy columns, battalion front, to within 100 yards; is met by the left, reinforced, supported by artillery,—in forty minutes the enemy flees, and Gen. Rains among their killed. The Unionists lost in killed 1,533, wounded 7,245.

Vicksburg attacked. Enemy's loss 4,560. Union loss 600 killed, 1,500 wounded, 1,000 missing.

The Arkansas Legislature enacts from $500 to $1,000 fine and imprisonment for from five to ten years, for trading with Yankees.

3d. Heavy skirmishing at Murfreesboro,

Contest all day at Moorfield, Virginia, between Imboden and Jenkins' rebel cavalry, and Col. Washburne.

4th. The engagement at Moorefield continues. The enemy are finally driven four miles.

The enemy retreated last night from Murfreesboro, and lost during the entire engagement 14,560 killed and wounded. U. S. loss, 92 officers killed, 384 wounded, 1,441 men killed, 6,861 wounded, and 1,300 taken prisoners. This victory clears Middle Tennessee of enemies and saves us from invasion.

5th. Gens. Thomas, McCook and Crittenden occupy Murfreesboro and its surroundings.

7th-8th. BATTLE OF SPRINGFIELD, Mo.—Gen. Marmaduke, with 5,000 rebels and 16 pieces of artillery, advances against Gen. E. B. Brown with 2,400 men and 5 pieces of artillery. After two days severe conflict, the enemy is defeated and retreats towards Arkansas. Union loss, 17 killed and a number wounded. Rebel loss, 300 killed, wounded and missing.

Capt. Moore, with 100 men, surprises 300 rebels at Hunter's Mills, killing 16, wounding 40, capturing 46 men and horses.

Lieut. Cushing, with 25 men, captures a fort on Little River, N. C. The enemy fled, leaving all as the Unionists enter.

9th. Wheeler's Mounted Rifles drive back the enemy under Gen. Pryor, on Blackwater.

10th. 700 Unionists attack 4,000 rebels and 5 guns at Hartzville, Mo., driving them 5 miles. The enemy return to Hartzville by a circuitous route, and the battle is renewed, and continues till sundown. Union loss, 35 killed and wounded. Confederate loss, about 150.... Federal steamers throw 167 shells into Galveston.

11th. BATTLE OF ARKANSAS POST, ARK. — Defended by over 5,000 rebels under Gen. Churchill. The Union forces under Gen. McClernand, and 4 gunboats under Porter, assault the works and finally destroy the fortifications, when the entire garrison surrenders, with 550 killed and wounded, 4,720 prisoners, 9 heavy guns, and all the stores and ammunition. Union loss, 129 killed, 31 wounded and 17 missing.

12th. Two Texas regiments march into Arkansas Post and are captured.

The rebels capture a brig. The captain's wife intoxicates the rebel crew and binds them in irons, and runs the brig into St. Thomas.

13th. Guerillas sink the steamer "Charter," with valuable stores near Nashville, capturing 16 men.

14th. The "Alabama" (C.S.) sinks the "Hatteras" in a naval conflict off Galveston.

17th. A Newbern expedition drives 1,800 rebels from Pollocksville, N. C.

18th. Des Arc, Duval's Bluff, and St. Charles, Arkansas, captured with 150 prisoners, 2 columbiads, 300 small arms and a quantity of ammunition.

19th. The bill authorizing $100,000,000 to pay the army and navy, approved by President Lincoln.

The steamer "Mary Crane" burnt on the Cumberland by guerillas, with $30,000 worth of stores.

20th. The Richmond Examiner says: "The pledge once deemed foolish by the South, that he would hold, occupy and possess, all the forts belonging to the U. S. Government, has been redeemed almost to the letter by Lincoln."

21st. The enemy capture the brig "Morning Light" and schooner "Velocity," 13 guns, $1,000,000 worth of property and 109 prisoners.

25th. Major Gen. Hooker succeeds Gen. Burnside in the command of the Army of the Potomac.

26th. 60 transports, 70,000 men and 150 schooners, with war material, leave Beaufort, N. C. for Port Royal.

27th. Col. Wyndham's Union cavalry defeats Stuart's cavalry at Middleburg, Va.

The Charleston Mercury says: "A force of 1.000 men from Gen. Kirby Smith's division, aided by companies collected in North Carolina, attacked their front and rear, killing many."

29th. 1,300 Unionists organized in Brownsville, Texas.

From 200 to 300 rebel sympathizers attempt to rescue a carload of rebel prisoners, at Chicago.

Gen. Corcoran, after cannonading the rebels 2½ hours, drives them from their position near Blackwater, then with fixed bayonets forces them back 3½ miles, their dead and wounded left on the field. Union loss, 24 killed, 80 wounded.

30th. The enemy captured at Stone River the gunboat "Isaac P. Smith," with 11 guns and 180 men, killing 8 and wounding 15.

31st. U. S. troops occupy Franklin, Tenn.

The blockading fleet off Charleston attacked by the gunboats "Palmetto State" and "Chicora," with three small vessels. The inner blockading line driven back for a time, but soon returns. The "Mercedita" and "Keystone State" disabled and 27 men killed.

Feb. 2d. Gen. Sloan orders the execution of all guerrillas, bushwhackers, and rebel recruiting officers in the District of Central Missouri.

Gunboat "New Era," at Island No. 10, attacked by 2,000 rebels last night, continuing till morning, when the enemy retired.

A rebel camp at Middleton, Tenn, surprised by Stokes' cavalry, killing 10, capturing 100, and their entire camp.

The bill to enlist negroes into the U. S. service passes the House of Representatives.

3d. Gen. Wheeler with 4,500 men, assaults the garrison at Fort Donelson, 800 strong under Colonel Harding, but is repulsed by the gunboats, losing 140 killed, 400 wounded, and 130 prisoners. Union loss, 126.

4th. Union cavalry drives Marmaduke's forces from Batesville, Arkansas.

5th. Morgan defeated by Gen. Reynolds at Alexandria....Dawson's entire guerrillas killed or captured at Dyersburg. Tennessee.

7th Gen. Reynolds' expedition returns to Murfreesboro, with 50 prisoners, including Gen. Anderson and Col. Martin, of the rebel Tennessee Legislature....Federal troops occupy Lebanon, Tenn., capturing over 600 of Morgan's men.

10th. Enemy routed at Lake Providence.

The gunboats "Queen of the West" and "De Soto" run by the batteries at Vicksburg.

11th. Over 600 Unionists from North Alabama and Mississippi. join the Federal army to escape rebel conscription. The rebels are forcing into the ranks all between the ages of 18 and 60.

12th. Gen. Grant cuts the Mississippi levees at Yazoo Pass and Greenville, Ark.

Col. Monroe with 250 troops, routs 500 of Morgan's cavalry, near Colinsville, Tennessee, killing 20, wounding a number, and capturing 6 men, 50 horses, and 300 stand of arms; 3 Unionists wounded.

The "Jacob Bell," with a cargo worth $1,500,000, captured and burnt by the privateer "Florida."

13th. The enemy defeated in a skirmish at Bolivar, Tennessee.

14th. The "Queen of the West" runs aground under the rebel batteries by the treachery of the pilot, at Gordon's Landing, on Red River, and captured with 50 prisoners.

17th. Representatives from 1st and 2d Districts of La., admitted to Congressional seats....The Richmond Examiner objects to the peace propositions of the French Minister of Foreign Affairs, and said the "only peace commissioners they had were Lee, Beauregard, Johnston, Longstreet and Jackson."....The bombardment of Vicksburg has commenced.

19th. Yazoo Pass expedition surprises and routes 200 rebel cavalry at Coldwater, killing 6, wounding 3, and capturing 15.

20th. Governor Andrew Johnson, of Tennessee, confiscates the rents and profits of all real estate and personal property of rebels for the use of the United States.

22d. The garrison at Richmond driven back by 700 rebel cavalry under Chenault, Tucker, and Cluke. The enemy leave, closely pursued; they are attacked and routed at Tuscumbia, capturing 200 prisoners, 1 piece of artillery, a quantity of ammunition and provisions.

24th. The enemy capture the iron-clad "Indianola" and crew, below Vicksburg..... The enemy repulsed in a cavalry engagement near Stafford, Va., losing 200 prisoners and many killed.

Fitzhugh Lee and Stuart's cavalry, in a raid on the Union picket lines at Kelly's Ford, are repulsed by reinforcements.

26th. 30,000 persons present at a Union meeting at Indianapolis, Indiana..... The Cherokee National Council abolishes the ordinance of secession forced upon them by intrigue.

27th. The enemy is dispersed in a skirmish at Yazoo Pass, with 6 killed and 25 prisoners; Union loss, 6 wounded.

March 1st. A severe conflict in which 2,000 cavalry and infantry drive a division of Morgan's cavalry from Bradyville, Tennessee, killing 8, wounding 30, capturing 9 officers and 80 privates, 300 saddles and official papers; Unionists lost about one-half as many as the rebels.

2d. Col. Rumble's troops kill two men, and capture 50 in a skirmish with guerrillas near Mt. Sterling, Ky.

3d. The Conscription Act approved by President Lincoln, having passed the Senate on the 16th, and the House on the 25th inst.

The monitors make the 4th attack on Fort McAllister.

The Union army engages Van Dorn's forces near Franklin, driving him back, killing 13 and losing but 2.

23 East Tennesseeans capture 50 rebel cavalrymen, near Nolinsville, Tenn.

5th. BATTLE OF SPRINGHILL, TENN.—General Van Dorn with 20,000 men, attacks General Coburn with 2,500 Unionists, and one battery. After a day's battle, the infantry's ammunition gives out, when all are killed or captured. About 65 killed and 250 wounded; rebels killed 180, wounded 450.

7th. General Minty's Union troops defeat Russell's cavalry at Unionville, Tennessee, with a loss of 50 killed, 180 wounded, and 58 prisoners.

9th. Mosby's forces captured at Fairfax Court House, Va.

General Banks' expedition, 18,000 strong, leaves New Orleans for Port Hudson.

10th. The 6th and 7th Illinois cavalry under Col. Grierson, surround and capture Richardson's guerrillas, near Covington, Tenn.

Col. Lee captures Gen. Looney and guerrillas at Wythe Depot near Germantown, Tenn.

A brigade of negro troops capture and occupy Jacksonville, Fla.

12th. Gen. Granger's forces, having driven Van Dorn across Duck River, return to Franklin, Tenn.

13th. The enemy attack Newburn, North Carolina, but are repulsed.

14th. PORT HUDSON, with 6,000 rebels under Gardner, bombarded by 15 vessels under Farragut, who retires after an action of 3 hours, with a loss of 65.... Immense Union meeting at the

Acadcmy of Music, New York.... Admiral Farragut passes Port Hudson with a part of his fleet; 6 killed and 9 wounded ...Admiral Porter, with 5 gunboats, leaves Yazoo River for the Upper Yazoo....... United States officers at San Francisco seize the schooner "Chapman," as being a privateer.

17th. Gen. Averill's cavalry, about 200 strong, charges the enemy's rifle-pits and intrenchments, capturing nearly the entire force. Fitzhugh Lee's cavalry, endeavoring to reinforce the rifle-pits, are driven back 4 miles in a hand-to-hand conflict, losing 80 prisoners.

18th. Grand Union meeting in Louisville, Ky.

The Unionists capture 46 prisoners and large stores without loss, on St. Francis' River..... Admiral Farragut passes Grand Gulf, under fire of 150 field-pieces, with 3 killed and 8 wounded.

20th. John Morgan, with 3,800 rebels, attacks 323 Union troops and 2 pieces of artillery, under Col. Hall, near Milton, Tennessee. After a terrific encounter of 4 hours, the enemy retires, leaving 50 killed 150 wounded, and 100 prisoners; Union loss, 7 killed and 31 wounded.

22d. Quantrell, with 200 guerrillas, puts 40 Union scouts to flight, killing 6 and 5 missing.

Gen. Grover reaches Baton Rouge with 350 bales of cotton, 1,500 hogsheads of sugar, 3,000 barrels of molasses, and 50 prisoners.

The enemy are beaten in a skirmish at Brashear City, Louisiana, and driven 8 miles, losing 10 killed, 20 wounded.

Blockade of Galveston.

24th. Danville, Kentucky, occupied by 3,000 rebels.

25th. A large detachment of Wheeler's rebel cavalry dash into Brentwood Station, Tennessee, and capture 200 infantry and their stores (these were afterwards retaken), with a loss of 10 killed and wounded, and 50 prisoners; Union loss, 16 killed. wounded and missing....The Confederates leave the banks of the Rappahannock....Skirmishes at Chantilly, in which 4 Unionists were killed and 39 captured....Unsuccessful attempt of the Federal rams "Lancaster" and "Switzerland," to run the batteries at Vicksburg.

27th. The rebel Pegram, having taken over 1,000 head of cattle, retreats from Stamford, Kentucky, but Col. Wolford presses him closely and retakes the cattle and 125 prisoners....Col. Montgomery's African brigade takes Pilatka, Florida, and 16 prisoners.

28th. A raid into the Kanawha Valley, by a detachment of Jenkins' cavalry.

29th. The enemy repulsed in an attack on Williamsburg. Va.

In a skirmish near Bolivar, Tennessee, 21 of Sol. Street's guerrillas are captured and himself wounded.

30th. Point Pleasant, Virginia, captured by 100 rebels, but subsequently driven out, losing 19 killed and 15 prisoners; Union loss, 2 killed and 3 wounded.

The forces under Pegram, Marshall, Cluke and Chenault, retreat from Kentucky, hotly pursued by Federal troops. Colonel Walford captures 200 of their cattle and 150 prisoners at Hall's Gap, and Col. Walker's 10th Kentucky cavalry attacks Cluke at Mt. Sterling, and drives his forces in confusion across the Licking River.... Enemy fortifying Chattanooga.

31st. BATTLE OF SOMERSET, KY.—Gen. Gilmore with 1,300 Union troops defeats Gen. Pegram's rebel force of 2,800, and drives them into the Cumberland, killing and wounding 50 and capturing 400, including 20 commissioned officers; Federal loss, 10 killed and 25 wounded.

April 1st. The enemy capture the gunboat "Diana" at Petersonville, La., killing and wounding a number, and parole 99 men.

2d. The Union troops under Gen. Hazen attempt to capture 1,200 rebels under Gen. Smith, but they being apprized, flee, and are pursued in a running engagement 3 miles, losing in killed and wounded 15, capturing 30 men and 50 horses, and a quantity of ammunition.... The Unionists, in an engagement at Drainville, lose 50 killed, wounded and missing.

2,000 Union cavalry, under Gen. Stanley, and Col. Matthew's infantry brigade, attack 8 regiments at Snow Hill, Tennessee, under Morgan and Wheeler, dispersing them in confusion, and killing about 20 and taking 60 prisoners and 300 horses.

4th. The enemy defeated in a skirmish at Nonconah, Tenn.

Hill and Pettigrew, with 10,000 rebels, surrounded Gen. Foster with a brigade and regiment of N. C. troops, at little Washington, North Carolina.... Federal troops defeat Richardson's guerrillas near Moscow, Tennessee, killing and wounding 28.

5th. Bread riots in Richmond, Va.

6th. 350 cavalry under Gen. Mitchell, scatter a rebel camp at Green Hill, Tennessee, killing 5 and capturing 15, with their equipage.

7th. Admiral Dupont, with the gunboat fleet, having 34 guns, makes an unsuccessful attack on FORT SUMTER, with 300 guns. The "Keokuk" is sunk. The fleet lost 2 killed and 13 wounded; the fort had six wounded.

Major Ransom, of the 6th Kansas, returns to Kansas City from a raid among the guerillas, having killed 34, destroyed 15 rebel camps, and a great quantity of munitions of war.

8th. 7,000 Union troops attempt to reinforce General Foster, at Little Washington, North Carolina, but are repulsed with a loss of 50.

9th. Col. Daniels, with 900 colored troops, takes Passagoula, Mississippi. A rebel force advancing is driven off with 20 killed and many wounded. The enemy being reinforced, the Unionists return to Ship Island.

10th. 300 rebels capture a car-train, including the mail, 100 passengers, and about 20 officers.

BATTLE OF FRANKLIN, TENN.—Gens. Van Dorn and Forrest, with 15,000 rebels, attacks Gen. Granger. After two hours hard struggle, the enemy retreat, leaving 300 dead; Union loss, 100 killed, wounded and missing.

21 rebels captured in a skirmish near Fort Donelson.

11th. Col. Streight's command leaves Nashville, Tenn., for a raid into Georgia.

13th. Gen. Wheeler captures two trains on the Nashville & Chattanooga Railroad, taking $30,000 and a number of Federal officers....The enemy is defeated in an engagement at Franklin, La.

14th. Gen. Banks, after two days' fighting, occupies New Iberia, La....Gen. Foster reinforced and provisioned.

15th. The enemy abandon the siege of Washington N. C.

16th. Admiral Porter's fleet of 7 gunboats and 3 transports, runs the Vicksburg batteries....The "Vanderbilt" captures the British steamer "Gertrude," with a quantity of gunpowder and military stores, attempting to run into Charleston.

17th. Col. Dills, with 200 of the 39th Kentucky, attack the enemy under Col. French, at Pikeville, Kentucky. After an hour's conflict, takes 73 prisoners, including 130 officers, 30 horses and a quantity of stores....The Federal batteries open on Vicksburg.

The Federal left at Suffolk attacked by 5,000 of the enemy, but repulsed by Fort Dix and driven 5 miles.

18th. 2,000 rebels and 6 guns taken on the Nansemond, Va.

3,000 rebels attack the garrison of 2,000 at Fayetteville, Ark. The enemy were repulsed, killing 5 and wounding 17.

19th. Col. Graham crosses the Cumberland and routs the enemy, killing 30.

20th. Marmaduke, with 2,000 rebels and 6 pieces of artillery, defeats 400 Unionists under Col. Smart, at Peterson, Mo. Union loss, 11 killed and 20 wounded; rebel loss, 140.

Large Union meeting in Baltimore.

21st. 30 rebels captured in a skirmish at Kelly's Ford.

Gen. Reynolds surprises and captures 130 rebels at McMinnville, Tenn....Congress petitioned by the Unionists of Louisiana, to form a State Government.

22d. The Selina expedition returns to Mumfordsville, Tennessee, having destroyed 100,000 pounds of bacon, 20,000 bushels of wheat and corn, and a great quantity of other stores, the town of Selina, and 60 rebel transport boats.

23d. Col. Morrill's Union forces take Port Royal, Virginia, driving out 200 rebel cavalry. These return reinforced, and the Unionists retreat to camp....The Federals occupy Tuscumbia, Alabama, driving the enemy out with a loss of 100.

24th. Frederickton occupied by rebels.

History of the Great Rebellion. 51

The Unionists, under Gen. Corcoran dislodge the enemy from their rifle-pits near Suffolk, and pursue them several miles.

Col. Grierson destroys 38 rebel car-loads of Quartermaster and commissary stores, at Newton Mills, Miss.... At Weber's Falls, Indian Territory, the enemy scattered, and equipage captured.

26th. Cape Girardeau, Mo., attacked by 8,000 rebels under Marmaduke, who are repulsed after two hours' conflict, with 275 killed and wounded, and many prisoners; Unionists, 6 killed and 6 wounded.... Col. Prince, of Grierson's advance, destroys 40 cars laden with all kinds of military stores.

27th. Col. Walker's Union cavalry surprise and rout a rebel camp on Carter's Creek, Tenn., killing 2, wounding 10, and capturing 138 men, 250 horses and mules.... Jenkins' guerrillas occupy Morgantown, Rawlesburg and Moorefield, Va.

28th. Gen. Dodge, at Tuscumbia, Alabama, repulses, after several hours' engagement, Gen. Forrest and Col. Roddy..... Col. Grierson captures and paroles 200 prisoners at Brookhaven, Miss.

29th. The Army of the Potomac, crossing the Rappahannock, surprise the pickets capturing 400. The left wing, 35,000 strong, crosses 4 miles below Fredericksbrug, and engages the enemy 12 hours, when he leaves his rifle-pits and retreats 8 miles.

The " Oneida," of New York, with a cargo worth $500,000, captured and burnt by the privateer ":Florida."

Bombardment of Grand Gulf, Miss., by 7 gunboats under Admiral Porter, with 26 killed and 54 wounded, who then runs the batteries.

30th. Imboden and Jones, with a large cavalry force, attack Col. Mulligan with 350 men at Fairmount, Va. The garrison surrenders with 1 killed and 4 wounded, after fighting most of the day. The enemy admit a loss of 100.... Chancellorsville occupied by Gen. Meade's corps.... The enemy's batteries on the Yazoo River attacked by Sherman's gunboats and transports.

Col. Streight's troops engage the enemy at Day's Gap, Alabama, killing and wounding about 70, and taking their artillery. At 3 P. M. another engagement commences, lasting till dark. The Federals spike the captured cannon, and leave in the night, having lost in the two skirmishes 3 killed and over 20 wounded.

May 1st. The enemy defeated in a skirmish at Thompson's Station, Tenn., with a loss of 14 killed, 20 wounded and 11 captured.

Gen. Stoneman, with a large cavalry force, leaves Falmouth on a raid to Lee's rear, to cut his communication with Richmond.

BATTLE OF MAGNALIA.—Part of Gen. Grant's forces of 25,000, and Pemberton's rebel army of 12,000 under Gen. Bowen, have an engagement. The rebels were defeated with a loss of 1,500 killed and wounded, and 500 prisoners; the Union troops lost 130 killed, 718 wounded, and 5 missing.... Three citizens and one soldier disperse 28 rebel cavalry, killing 5 and capturing all their horses, and equipments and money, in Wayne County, Ky.

2d. Col. Grierson, with 2,000 cavalry, reaches Baton Rouge, having traveled over 800 miles, in 15 days; fought and dispersed all rebels that they met, capturing 1,000 prisoners, 1,200 horses, and destroyed over $4,000,000 worth of property.

BATTLE OF CHANCELLORSVILLE.—After 3 days skirmishing, Gen. Lee, with about 90,000 rebels, attacks Gen. Hooker, with about 100,000 men, with a degree of success. Schulz's division, of the 11th corps receiving the first terrific crash of musketry, from Jackson's overwhelming numbers, broke and fled, losing 12 pieces of artillery. Capt. Bert's batteries and Berry's division of the 3d corps stays the onrolling current of the enemy, till reinforced. Gen. Sickles cuts the enemy's column, and his communication with the main army being broken, owing to the 11th retreating, a night attack is made at 11 o'clock and the rebels give back. Sickles brings off 400 prisoners. The Union lines being restored, fall back to Chancellorsville The days' conflict was terrific and telling on both sides, and the exhausted armies repose on their arms, awaiting the unknown events of the morrow.

3d. The engagement reopens at 5½ A. M., and continues with terrific carnage until 11½. The enemy makes a number of efforts to break the Union lines, but are checked by Gen. Berry's division, the heroes of Slocum and Sickles force death into their faltering ranks. The divisions of A. P. Hill, McLaws and Anderson, are added to Jackson's corps, but the Union troops with bayonets hold their ground for nearly an hour, and then fall back to intrenchments. Gen. Sedgwick storms and carries Marye's Hill, held by Early's division, and then takes the Heights of Fredericksburg, driving the enemy to Lee's rear, between himself and Hooker, capturing 17 guns and nearly 1,000 prisoners. Then forces and drives the enemy from Salem Heights. Lee now recovers Chancellorsville and drives Hooker 1½ miles. In the Chancellorsville conflict, Gen. Stonewall Jackson mortally wounded—Hooker insensible from the shock of a cannon ball and the army without a head for one hour—one cause of no better success. U. S. loss, from 10,000 to 15,000 killed, wounded and missing; C. S. loss, as estimated by Gen. Hooker, killed and wounded, 18,000, 5,000 prisoners. Admiral Porter and Gen. Grant captures Grand Gulf, 50 prisoners and a large quantity of stores....Rebel Gens. Forrest and Roddy capture Col. Streight's entire command, of 1,375 men, horses and equipments, near Rome, Ga. Col. Streight, in his entire raid, lost 72 men in killed, wounded and missing. The enemy from 500 to 600.

4th. Fredericksburg retaken by Lee, and Sedgwick's brave forces retreat losing near one-third of their number....Col. Kilpatrick, of Stoneman's command, penetrates the fortifications of Richmond within 5 miles of the city.

5th. C. L. Vallandigham arrested....Rebel camp at Pitty's Mills, North Carolina, surprised; 14 men, 36 horses, and the entire camp taken....Admiral Porter captures Fort De Russy on Red River....Heavy reinforcements reaching Lee; he advances on Hooker, and after a bloody battle is driven back across the Rappahannock. The Union loss in these Chancellorsville battles, 17,197 Siege of Suffolk abandoned..Admiral Porter takes Alexandria, La.

7th. West Point, Va. occupied by Gen. Keyes....The rebel Gen. Van Dorn killed by Dr. Peters of Tenn.

8th. Bombardment of Port Hudson commences.

9th. The enemy defeated in a skirmish at Horseshoe Bend on the Cumberland.

12th. 6,000 Unionists under Gen. McPherson, after two hours' severe conflict, take Raymond, Miss., defended by 7,000 rebels, under Gen. Gregory. The rebels lost in killed, wounded and missing, 969; U. S. killed 69, wounded 341, missing 30....Over 100 rebels surprised at Linden, Tennessee....30 men and 7 officers captured, including 50 horses, arms and stores, by 55 men of the West Tennessee cavalry.

13th. Gen. Schofield assumes command in Mo....Col. Hatch's raid into Alabama results in the capture of 400 prisoners and 600 horses.

14th. Gen. Grant, with about 15,000 troops, after 3 hours' engagement, takes Jackson, Miss., defended by 10,000 rebels under Joe Johnson. Union loss, 40 killed, 240 wounded and 6 missing; the enemy lost in killed and wounded 450....Gens. Gregg and Walker defeated at Mississippi Springs by Gen. Grant....Clinton, Miss., taken by Gen. McPherson.

15th. Enemy defeated with heavy loss at Beaver Dam Church, Va....Skirmishing around Suffolk, Va....Col. Clayton's expedition of the 6th ult., reaches Helena, having defeated the enemy in two battles, killing and wounding 150, destroying $100,000 worth of military stores, with a loss of 2 killed and 8 wounded.

16th. BATTLE OF CHAMPION HILL.—Gen. Grant, with 20,000 men, engages Lieut. General Pemberton with 25,000. The enemy, after a severe conflict from 7 A. M. to 3 P. M., are defeated with 2,500 killed and wounded, 1,500 prisoners, and 29 pieces of artillery; Federal loss, 426 killed, 1,842 wounded, and 289 missing.

17th. BATTLE OF BLACK RIVER.—Gen. McClernand, with about 10,000 Unionists, encounter Gen. Pemberton with 8,700, defeats and drives him into Vicksburg, killing and wounding about 600, capturing 2,000 men and 17 pieces of artillery. Union loss, 29 killed, 242 wounded, 4 missing.

18th. The Union troops in the various encounters to this time, in the advance on Vicksburg, captured 9,000 prisoners, and 68 pieces of artillery....Siege of Vicksburg commences with 30,000 men under General Grant, and 5 or 6 gunboats under Admiral Porter.

19th. Richmond, Missouri, plundered by rebel guerrillas....Maj. Gen. Foster, of the Department of North Carolina, enjoins all his officers to assist in recruiting colored volunteers.

20th. The outer works of Vicksburg taken, with 57 pieces of artillery and many prisoners....Admiral Porter destroys at Yazoo City the enemy's navy yard and works, and 3 large steamers, all valued at $2,000,000....Col. Phillips defeats Price's advance at Fort Gibson, Ark., with severe loss.

21st. Vallandigham ordered beyond the Federal lines....Plattsburg, Mo., plundered, and $11,000 State money taken by rebel guerrillas....Gen. Grant captures and turns the enemy's batteries north of Vicksburg on the city, and Admiral Porter silences the river batteries....Gen. Augur's division, of Banks' command, effectually defeats the enemy near Port Hudson, they fleeing into the intrenchments, leaving on the ground many dead and wounded, and over 1,000 prisoners. Union loss, 12 killed and 56 wounded.

22d. In an engagement at Gum Swamp, North Carolina, the Unionists defeat and drive the enemy from their intrenchments, wounding 7 and capturing 195 prisoners, 1 gun, and 50 horses and mules. Federal loss, 1 killed, 7 wounded.....Major Walker, with 2,000 men from the 5th Kansas and 3d Iowa cavalry, defeats and drove 400 guerillas near Helena, killing 9 and wounding 21; Union loss, 4 killed and 20 wounded....Gen. Grant repulsed with a loss of 1,000 men in an assault on Vicksburg....Gen. Pemberton proposes to surrender Vicksburg, provided the Confederates be permitted to lay down their arms and march out. Proposition refused, and the siege vigorously prosecuted.

24th. The Federals, in an encounter at Senatobia, Mississippi, defeat the enemy, killing 19, wounding 20, and capturing 60 prisoners.

26th. Guerrilla camp near Memphis broken up.....Gen. Banks and Augur invest Port Hudson.

27th. The siege of Port Hudson La. commences. The fleet, under Admiral Farragut, bombards in front, and the land forces, 25,000 strong, under Gen. Banks, assault the rebel intrenchments, in the rear, defended by 10,000 rebels under Gen. Gardner. The outer line of works is taken, after losing about 900 killed, wounded and missing. Rebel authorities give their entire loss at 600.

29th. The 8th Illinois cavalry and Peninsula Scouts, capture 125 prisoners, 1,500 contrabands, 800 horses, and destroy 4 smuggling routes.

30th. 600 wagons, 3,000 horses and mules, 1,500 cattle, and 6,000 negroes reach New Orleans, having abandoned Teche County, Louisiana.

31st. 200,000 percussion caps found on 12 rebels, endeavoring to reach Vicksburg....Chicago Times suppressed.

June 1st. Gen. Kilpatrick's raiding party reaches Urbana, Va., having captured 300 horses and mules, 1,000 contrabands, and destroyed $2,000,000 worth of property....Col. Cornyn's expedition reaches Corinth, having defeated Roddy and captured 100 prisoners, 600 horses and mules, 200 contrabands, and destroyed immense rebel stores.

4th. The garrison at Franklin, Tenn., attacked, by 200 rebels and are repulsed with heavy loss. 3,000 Union troops under Gen. Kimball, defeat after 30 minutes' fight, Wirt Adams, with 2,000 rebels, at Sartalia, Miss., killing and wounding a number, and capturing 100 prisoners. Union loss, 17.

5th. 3,600 shells thrown into Vicksburg in one hour.....General Kilpatrick reaches head-quarters with 500 horses and 250 contrabands....1,200 rebels attack a detachment of Grierson's cavalry near Port Hudson, killing 30, and capturing 40 prisoners, and 60 horses.....Lee's army commences moving northward.

6th. The Chief of the Cherokees, John Ross, offers 1,200 loyal Indians to the U. S. Government.

The colored troops repulse the Confederates at Gann's Point, Milliken Bend. killing and wounding, 200 ; Union loss, 78 killed, and 370 wounded.

7th. 400 Union cavalry rout two Confederate regiments at Raccoon Ford, on the Rapidan, killing 5 and wounding 15...... Colonel Wilder brakes up a guerrilla band at Liberty, Tennessee, capturing 62 prisoners, 320 mules and horses, arms, equipage, etc., and retreats to Murfreesboro..... *Battle of Beverly Ford, Va.* 12,000 of Stuart's cavalry, with 16 pieces of artillery, engage 9,000 Unionists in a saber combat, under Pleasanton, from 5 A. M., to 3 P. M., when the enemy, driven back about 4 miles, are reinforced. Pleasanton retreats with a loss of about 400 men ; enemy's total loss, 759.

10th. The Unionists, after two hours' hard fighting near Monticello, defeat the enemy, losing 30 killed and wounded....Large force of Texans repulsed at Lake Providence.

11th. It is estimated 50,000 colored troops, to this date, have enrolled in the U. S. service. ...The " Peace Party," or rebel sympathisers, nominate Vallandigham for Governor of Ohio..... General R. B. Mitchell's cavalry, being attacked at Triune, Tenn., by 5,000 Confederate cavalry, under Forest, and two batteries, defeats and drives them six miles, losing 21 killed and 70 wounded and prisoners....Leading citizens of Louisiana declare to the President a willingness to make " That State a part of the Union, as before rebellion."

12th. A government train, 200 horses, etc., taken by the Confederates in a raid on Elizabethtown, Ky.

13th. Grant within 20 yards of the enemy's works at Vicksburg ; the bombardment prosecuted with vigor, and Confederate batteries mostly silenced......Lee moving toward Pennsylvania with a force of about 98,000.

14th. General Ewell with 18,000 Confederates nearly surrounds General Milroy with 6,500 Unionists, at Winchester, and carries his outer works..... General Banks storms the enemy's works at Port Hudson with partial success, gaining a position within about 75 yards of the fortification ; losing, killed and wounded, 700 men...... The Army of the Potomac moves to counteract Lee's operations in the Shenandoah Valley.

15th. General Milroy spikes his guns and evacuates Winchester : 4 miles off, coming in contact with the enemy, cuts his way through ; losing in killed, wounded and missing, 1,800 men, 3 batteries of artillery, 6,000 muskets, 280 wagons, etc. Enemy's loss, killed, wounded and missing, 850 ... The enemy occupy Harper's Ferry, but are shelled out from Maryland Heights by General Tyler....... The enemy surround and compel Colonel Smith, at Hagerstown, to surrender, after 1½ hours' hard fighting...... The Unionists defeat the enemy in Fleming Co., Ky., losing 15 killed and 50 wounded.... General Elliott's marine brigade, 2,300 strong, drives 3,500 Confederates out of Richmond, La., capturing 30 prisoners, and burn the town.

17th. The enemy, at Port Hudson, capture the 4th and 6th Wisconsin Regiments while making an assault on that place.

18th. 300 Confederate cavalry burn 6 steamers and 75 bales of cotton in Plaquerine, La.... Harrisburg, Penn., fortified.... 3,000 Confederates occupy Hagerstown.... 200 of the 4th Kentucky (rebel) cavalry cross the Ohio river into Indiana : a skirmish ensues at Orleans with Mitchell's Home Guard, killing 3 and wounding 20 of the Guard—the raiders pursued.

19th. Only two of the Kentucky raiders return ; 54 were captured ; the remainder, either killed or drowned.... McConnellsburg, Penn., plundered ; $12,000 worth of cattle driven off by Jenkens', Confederates.... Gen. Kilpatrick's cavalry and Stewart's (rebel) advance engage each other all day at Middleburg. Stewart repulsed in every charge and finally driven from the field. Enemy's cavalry reaches Gettysburg.

21st. Carter with 3,000 cavalry in east Tennessee, on a raid, captures 500 prisoners, 1,000 stand of arms, 200 boxes of amunition, 3 pieces of artillery, and also does great damage to railroads and bridges.... Vicksburg terrifically cannonaded.

23d. *Battle of Big Black, Miss.*—Johnston's forces attack Gen. Osterhaus ; after a long and severe conflict the enemy is greatly cut up and retreats, leaving 18 guns and 1,500 prisoners ; Union loss, 29 killed and 242 wounded..... Pittsburg, Penn., fortified.

24th. Enemy occupy Chambersburg, Penn.... The Union loss 50 killed and wounded in an engagement at Bridgeport, Miss.... 71 of the 9th Kansas are attacked at Westport, Mo., by 200 guerrillas, under Quantrell and Parker ; 26 marauders killed and 6 wounded.

25th. The Unionists lose 55 killed and wounded in a conflict at Guy's Gap, Tenn..... Cleburne's division has a severe encounter with Willich's, Wilder's and Carter's brigades at Liberty Gap, Tenn. The enemy defeated with heavy loss after an

hour's engagement. Union loss, 40 killed and 100 wounded.
....Jeff Davis calls upon Alabama for 70,000 men to prevent that State from invasion...... In a skirmish at McConnellsburg, Penn., the Unionists draw back before superior numbers..... The Unionists evacuate Carlisle, Penn.

26th. Early's command occupies Gettysburg, Penn., and General Rhoades' division, Chambersburg...... The 11th Penn. Cavalry, under Col. Spear, takes 111 prisoners, including General W. F. H. Lee, 310 mules, 35 wagons, and 75 horses, with a loss of 3 killed and 8 wounded.... The enemy 1,500 strong, under Dick Taylor, retakes Berwick's Bay and the garrison of about 2,000 at Brashear City, La., and captures 1,800 prisoners, 30,000 rounds of amunition, 30 pieces of artillery, $30,000 worth of sutler's and medical stores, and butchers, in cold blood, at the Contraband Camp, near Brashear City, 3,000 old men, women and children, and occupes all Louisiana west of the Mississippi.... General Meade supersedes General Hooker in command of the Army of the Potomac.... Carlisle, Penn., occupied by the enemy, their advance reaching within 13 miles of Harrisburg....The Federals capture 3,000 rebels at Hoover's Gap, Tenn.

28th. Pennsylvania thoroughly aroused by rebel invasion...... General Stanley defeats and captures 750 rebels, drives 100 into the river at Guy's Gap and Shelbyville. Union loss, 6 killed and 30 wounded... General Green, with 3,000 Confederates, attacks Donaldsonville, La., at 1 A. M., and continues till daylight, when he is repulsed with 64 killed, 16 wounded and 170 prisoners. Union loss, 6 killed and 16 wounded.

29th. Rosecrans' strategy causes Bragg to abandon his fortifications and fall back to Tullahoma.... General Lee and staff at Carlisle Penn., and collect $30,000 worth of provisions.... The rebels attack the Union garrison, at Lake Providence, driving them into their entrenchments, killing and wounding 50, when they are repulsed by the arrival of gunboats.

30th. Pleanton's cavalry occupies Gettysburg, driving the enemy off....40,000 Confederates and 40 pieces of artillery move from Carlisle to Gettysburg, and the Unionists cut their line by occupying York and Hanover....Enthusiastic war meeting in Indianopolis.

July 1st. *Battle of Gettysburg, Penn.*—About 97,000 Unionists, under General Meade, and about 120.000 under General Lee, opens at 9 A. M., by Longstreet and Hill's Confederate forces attacking the 1st and 11th Corps. The 1st Corps, being in advance, sustains the terific onslaught of the enemy till reinforced. Here the gallant Reynolds falls. Heavy skirmishing during the day, and the Union troops are driven into the strong position of Cemetry Hill....Union forces occupy Carlisle, Penn., driving the enemy out..... A severe cavalry encounter at Hanover, Penn., lasting near the entire afternoon; Union loss, about 200; rebel loss, 400 killed, wounded and prisoners, and 6 pieces of artillery. ......General Rosecrans' advance marches on Tullahoma—Bragg evacuated last night.

2d. *The Battle of Gettysburg* reopens at 4 P. M., by a heavy and terrific artillery duel, in which the entire forces of Longstreet and Hill, 45,000 strong, are precipitated on Meade's left but recoil beneath the overpowering strength of the loyal forces. Again the enemy deal a severe stroke on Meade's extreme right and hold their position, in defiance of all resistance, with a loss of near 6,000 prisoners.... A severe battle near Tullahoma, Tenn., lasting from daylight till 2 P. M., when the enemy retreat, leaving 2,000 prisoners. Union loss, 1,100.

3d. *The Battle of Gettysburg* resumed at 1 P. M., and continues with fearful carnage till 4 P. M., the enemy seem determined, as by a will of destiny, to drive our forces from Cemetry Hill. On they tread, dealing out and receiving death, but being unsuccessful they at last assault our left center, again and again, but the gallant loyal forces prove invincible to perhaps the most terrific charges of the war; and the enemy, no longer able to withstand the iron storm of death, retire amid terrible slaughter. Enemy's loss, killed, wounded and missing, about 23,000; prisoners, 13,621; total, 36,621. Union loss, 2,837 killed; 13,718 wounded; 6,643 prisoners. Total, 23,198. Doubtless the most important battle of the war....McCook occupies Winchester, Decherd, and Cowan, Tenn., losing about 1,000 killed, wounded and prisoners, and taking about 4,000 prisoners.

4th. The day enthusiastically celebrated throughout the loyal States.....General Meade occupies Gettysburg.....General Kilpatrick captures and burns about 300 wagons and runs off the horses of Ewell's train, near Hagerstown, Md......Vicksburg—the Gibralter of the West—surrenders, including 19 Major and Brigadier-Generals, 4,000 field, line and staff officers, 90 siege guns, 128 field pieces, 35,000 muskets and rifles, and 80 stand of colors. Entire Confederate loss during the siege, from May 18th to July 4th, about 27,000. The officers are permitted to have their horses and 4 days' rations, and the men are paroled. The garrison had subsisted 4 days on mule meat. 2,500 persons killed in the city during the siege; 1,200 women and children living in caves. Entire Union loss at the siege, from May 18th to July 4th, 245 killed; 3,688 wounded; 303 missing. Gettysburg and Vicksburg are twin victories to the North—twin disasters to the South. Confederate money depreciates 1,000 per cent.... 4,000 rebels, under Morgan, defeat 200 Federals, after three and a half hours' fighting, near Green River bridge. Union loss, 6 killed, and 23 wounded and prisoners, Enemy's loss, 50 killed and 200 wounded......*Battle of Helena, Ark.*—10,000 rebel troops, under Generals Holmes,

Price and Marmaduke, engage 4,000 to 5,000 Federal troops, under General Prentiss, from 4 to 10 A. M. The contest is very severe, resulting in killing and wounding about 1,500 rebels and taking 1,130 prisoners, and 2 pieces of artillery. Union loss, about 230, killed and wounded.

5th. The enemy abandon their dead and wounded and retreat to Chambersburg and Greencastle, Penn......4,000 of Morgan's cavalry, after 7 hours' conflict, compel Colonel Hanson, with 500 Unionists, to surrender......10 men of the 63d Indiana, defeats 90 rebel cavalry near Lebanon, Ky.....General Sherman engages and defeats Johnson's forces near Big Black, taking 2,000 prisoners.

6th. General Gregg engages the enemy at Fayetteville, Penn., and takes 4,000 prisoners..... General Lee's army utterly routed and retreating towards the Potomac—Meade in pursuit......Gen. Grant reports his losses at Vicksburg, and preceding battles, at 1,243, killed, 7,095 wounded, and 537 missing.

7th. Lee's army, retreating, reaches Hagerstown, Md....Rosecrans occupies Tallahoma—Bragg retreating.

8th. Port Hudson, Miss., defended by 5,500 Confederates, under General Gardner, being under siege since May by 2,000 Unionists, under General Banks, surrenders 5,500 prisoners, 2 steamers, 20 pieces of heavy artillery, 31 pieces of field artillery, 150,000 rounds of cartridges, and 44,800 pounds of cannon powder, etc ..Morgan with 4,800 rebels, 5,000 horses, and 4 pieces of artillery, crosses the Ohio river and invades Indiana.... Gen. Grant promoted to Major-General, and Gen. Meade to Brigadier in the Regular Army.

9th. Morgan's forces capture Corydon and Seymour, Indiana, and the border counties placed under martial law....Gen. Banks occupies Port Hudson....Union cavalry have destroyed over 500 wagons of Gen. Lee's retreating trains.

10th. Morgan occupies Salem, Greenville, Raoli, Vienna, Lexington, and Paris, Ind., damaging railroads, bridges and depots. ....Attack on Charlestown, 27 iron-clads and 25 transports open fire on the fortifications of Morris Island for three and a half hours, by which Gilmore secures a landing and erects batteries againts forts Wagner and Gregg. The Unionist's loss, 150 killed, wounded and captured. Enemy's loss, 200 killed and wounded, 11 heavy guns, and large quantities of camp equippage.

11th. Fort Wagner assaulted by three regiments under General Strong, and the flag unfurled over the fort, but not being properly supported, the assaulting party retire, losing about 350 killed, wounded and prisoners.....Indiana intensely excited, the militia ordered out.

12th. General Love of the Indiana Legion, marches against a detachment of Morgan's forces at North Vernon, who decamps..... Riot begins at New York, opposing the Conscription.

13th. 20 persons killed by the rioters, much excitement in New York....Morgan enters Ohio, destroying railroads, etc..... Col. Kise's militia engage and capture 20 rebels near Mitchell, Ind. .....Federalists occupy Hagerstown, the enemy falling back to Williamsport....Unionists disperse the rebels at Jackson, Tenn., killing, wounding and capturing 200 ; also, 250 horses and their artillery, and 500 conscripts.....Gen. Herron with 5,000 Unionists and 4 gun-boats, under Lieut. Walker, takes Yazoo City, defended by 800 men under Gen. Johnston, and take 250 prisoners. ....In the English House of Commons, Mr. Roebuck withdraws his motion for the recognition of the Southern Confederacy.

14th. General Lee crosses the Potomac, pressed by Kilpatrick's Union cavalry, capturing 1,500 prisoners, 3 battle flags, artilery, etc......Over 100 rioters killed by the military in N. Y. city. ......Rosecrans takes about 4,000 prisoners.

15th. The riot subsiding in N. Y......*Battle of Honey Springs, Ark.*—3,500 Unionists, and two batteries under Gen. Blunt, engage 6,000 rebels, and 4 pieces of artillery under Cooper, from 9 and a half A. M., to 1 and three-quarters P. M., when the enemy retreat with a loss of about 150 killed and 77 prisoners, and near 400 wounded, 400 stand of arms, and a 12-pound howitzer. Union loss, 17 killed and sixty wounded.

A Union cavalry force destroys Wyetteville, Va., wounding 75 and capturing 120 prisoners, 3 pieces of artillery and 70 small arms. Union loss, 65 killed and wounded.

16. Piketon, Ohio, surrenders to Morgan......Lee's army near Winchester, Va., having suffered immense loss in killed, wounded, prisoners and desertion, by its Penn. raid......The Mississippi river opened from St. Louis to New Orleans—having been closed for two years.

17th. Morgan being surrounded near Gallipolis, Ohio, escapes with part of his forces.

18th. Gen. Meade in pursuit of Gen. Lee crosses the Potamac. The 3d battalion of the 5th Ohio cavalry, and part of the 66th Illinois, surprise and capture between 3,000 and 4,000 rebels near Rienyi, Miss..... Fort Wagner furiously bombarded, and the works assaulted, ending in a repulse and severe carnage on both sides. Union loss, from the 10th, 1,000 ; Beauregard's 500 killed and 231 wounded......Admiral Porter reports the Red River expedition as capturing the Confederate steamers " Louisville " and " Elmira," 15,724 rounds of ammunition, 10,000 Enfield's cartridges, 52 hogsheads of sugar, 10 puncheons of rum, and great quantities of other stores.

19th. An unsuccessful attempt to drive the Unionists from James' Island....All of Morgan's men captured near Bealsville but about 1,500, who, escaping, near Pomeroy, Ohio, was attacked and 40 men killed and their artillery taken.

20th. Gen. Shackelford engaged Morgan from 3 to 4 P. M., capturing nearly all of his remaining force......Gen. Lee moves up the Valley......Gen. Gilmore commences the siege of Fort Wagner......A Newburn, N. C., expedition is estimated to have injured the enemy $5,000,000.

22d. Lee retreats to Winchester.

23d. 15 of Morgan's men killed and several wounded near Muskingum, Ohio......800 of Gen. Spinald's Excelsior Brigade drive about 2,400 of Longstreet's forces, with 17 pieces of artillery, near Manassass Gap at the point of the bayonet, killing, wounding and capturing about 500..... Gen. Gilmore reports 635 killed and wounded, and about 350 missing.

24th. Gen. Meade encounters the enemy at Port Royal, killing and wounding 2,300 ..... Gen. Rosecran's report of advance on Tullahoma and Manchester shows 85 killed, 462 wounded, and 13 missing, 1,575 prisoners; also, 59 commanding officers and large quantities of stores.

25th. The Confederate army moves towards Culpepper and Orange Court-house.

26th. Hon. John J. Crittenden dies at Frankfort, Ky...... Morgan loses 240 men in an engagement with 250 of the 9th Michigan cavalry......Gen. Shackelford captures John Morgan and remaining forces near New Lisbon, Ohio.

28th. Grant pursues Johnson beyond Pearl river.......Pegram with 2,500, men and 6 pieces of artillery, after an hour's hard conflict, drives the Union garrison from Richmond, Ky.

29th. The enemy defeated in an engagement near Lexington, Tenn., losing their colonel, 27 prisoners, and 2 pieces of artillery. ......2,500 of Pegram and Scott's forces engage in a severe contest the Union forces for two hours, when they retreat toward Winchester, Ky., pursued by Union cavalry......500 guerrillas captured near Helena, Ark.

30th. Morgan, Cluke and 28 others, confined in the Ohio Penitentiary...... Col. Saunders, after an hour's hard struggle, drives Pegram and Scott's (rebel) forces from Winchester toward Irvine; here they are encountered and defeated by the 14th Ky., with a loss of 7 killed, 18 wounded, and 75 captured......The rebel Richardson demands all able-bodied citizens in West Tennessee, between 18 and 45, to repair to his head-quarters, under pain of death—no distinction of property......Scott's (rebel) forces burn 60 wagons near Stamford, Ky., but are defeated near Somerset and driven in confusion to Lancaster, killing and wounding 20, and capturing 181.

August 2d. The iron-clads within 500 yards of fort Sumter and 500 prisoners taken on Folly Island, after a short resistance...... After a fierce encounter the "Ironsides," with the works on Morris' Island, silence the rebel batteries.

3d. Col. Spear reports having charged and defeated the enemy at Jackson, taking 76 prisoners, 60 bales of cotton, and 100 horses.

4th. 6,000 of Stuart's cavalry engage 3 brigades of Union troops and 13 pieces of artillery, from 2 P. M., until night at Brandy Station. Va., when the enemy retreat with 6 killed and 18 wounded.

5th. Great numbers of Tennessee refugees arriving in Ky.

7th, Gen. Sibly reports having 3 desperate conflicts with 2,200 Sioux Indians, driving them across the Missouri river, killing and wounding 150 and taking their equipments.

11th. An expedition from Natchez to Woodville, Miss., destroys $2,000,000 of property...... Union meeting in Washington, N. C.

12th. A letter from Robert Toombs exposes the bankruptcy of the Southern Confederacy.

13th. The enemy under Col. Coffee, attack the 7th State Militia at Pineville, Mo., but are repusled with 100 killed and wounded and many prisoners, arms, horses and cattle taken.

14th. General Gilmore opens on fort Sumter with 200-pound parrots.

15th. Terrific bombardment of Sumter.

16th. Gen. Rosecrans *en route* for Chattanooga...... General Burnside leaves Camp Nelson for Tennessee.

17th. The 9th Illinois, under Lieut.-Colonel Phillips, attacks and drives 2,000 rebels with 3 pieces of artillery, under Gen. Skinner, from Grenada, destroying 57 locomotives, over 400 cars, depot buildings, machine shops, and a large quantity of ordinances and commissary stores...... Terrific bombardment all day of fort Sumter. The fleet, under Admiral Dahlgreen, silences Wagner and nearly fort Gregg.

19th. Fort Sumter crumbling under Gilmore's batteries.

21st. The notorious Quantrel, with about 800 guerrillas, surprise the defenceless citizens of Lawrence, Kansas, at 4 A. M., setting the town on fire, consuming 182 houses, killing 190 persons, many of whom were women and children, and wounding about 600 more. After destroying over $2,000,000 of property, ransacking the place and committing the greatest atrocities, they flee, closely pressed by the infuriated Kansans, led by Gen. J. H. Lane...... Chattanooga shelled by Col. Wilder—Rosecrans' advance...... Price and Marmaduke's forces, about 35,000 strong, collected at Bayou Meteor, Ark...... Gen. Burnside's army moves from Crab Orchard, Ky., for Tennessee.

23d. Gen. Blunt, with 6,000 men and 12 pieces of artillery, crosses the Arkansas, defeats and pursues 11,000 rebels under Cooper and Steele, leaving their effects...... Fort Sumter almost demolished, after 7 days' bombardment.

24th. Gen. Jeff. Thompson, staff, and a 100 officers and men, captured at Pocahontas, Ark...... Quantril's guerrillas overtaken near Harrisonville, Mo.; over 60 killed and a considerable quan-

tity of the goods retaken that they captured at Lawrence......
Three men killed in a Copperhead riot at Danville, Illinois.
25th. Gen. Davidson drives out Marmaduke with 3,000 cavalry and 2 pieces of artillery, and occupies Brownville, Arkansas.
27th. Gen. Davidson, with 8,000 men, engages the entire day, 7,000 Confederates strongly posted at Bayou Meteor Bridge.
28th. *The Battle of Bayou Meteor Bridge* reopens early this morning and continues till noon, when the enemy flee, losing 100 killed and wounded, 300 prisoners. Union loss, 39 killed and wounded.
31st. Rosecrans' army invests Chatanooga......The monitors engage forts Moultrie, Gregg and Battery Bee, for three hours and retire.
September 1st. Colonel Cloud defeats 4,000 Confederates and takes fort Smith, Arkansas.
2d. Kingston, Tenn., taken by Burnside......Shackelford's brigade defeats Buckner and Pegram's (rebel) forces at London Bridge, Tenn.. killing and wounding 50; one Unionist wounded.
3d. 400 lodges of hostile Indians, in Dakota Territory, surprised and defeated by the Northwest Expedition, killing 300 and capturing 300 ; Union loss, 40 killed and wounded.
4th. Burnside occupies Knoxville, Tenn., amid great enthusiasm. ....Bread riot at Mobile.
6th. Beauregard orders fort Wagner evacuated, after 52 hours' insessent bombardment... .. Quantril's camp and stores destroyed and 2 killed, at Sinabar, Mo., by Capt. Coleman of the 9th Kan.
7th. Gilmore takes fort Wagner, 75 men and 36 guns......Col. Hayne's Confederates, capture 300 Federalists in an engagement at Limestone Station, Tenn......Col. Cloud, with 500 Cavalry and 1 battery, defeats Cabell, with 2,000 Confederates, in the Indian Territory.
8th. Capt. F. H. Stevens, with 20 boats, 34 officers, and 293 sailors, 120 mariners attempts to siege fort Sumter, but is repulsed. Total Union loss, 117......Gen. Franklin's Expedition, in an attack on Sabine City, Texas, repulsed with loss of two gunboats.
9th. The rebel Gen. Frazer with 2,000 men, being surrounded by 8,000 Unionists under Burnside, surrenders Cumberland Gap, Tenn., with 2,000 men, 14 pieces of artillery, 40 wagons, 200 mules, and a large quantity of commissary stores......The 2d Georgia (rebel) regiment destroys the office of the Raleigh (N. C.) "Standard," for opposing the Confederacy..... Jackson, with 1,800 Confederates, captures a detachment of the 100th Ohio at Tilford, Tenn.. after 3 hours' stubborn resistance, with a loss of 300 killed, wounded and captured......Crittenden's advance occupies Chattanooga at 1 P. M., Bragg evacuating the day and night previous.
10th. Little Rock, Ark., occupied by Gen. Steele, who lost 20 killed and wounded. Gen. Davidson pursues the enemy South.

...... Citizens destroy the office of the Raleigh (N. C.) "State Journal" in retaliation of the destruction of the "Standard" office.

11th. In a skirmish at Moorefield, W. Va., 15 Confederates were killed and 150 captured.

13th. The writ of *habeas corpus* suspended by President Lincoln, in cases of military arrests...... The enemy driven through Culpepper by Gen. Pleasanton's cavalry, capturing 5 guns and 104 men...... 5,300 Unionists, under Neglee, are attacked by 16,000 Confederates at Bird's Gap, Georgia, and driven three and a half miles, with a loss of 35 killed, wounded, and missing. He afterwards, however, retakes his ground.

15th. In a struggle for Morris' Island, the enemy report a loss of 700 men.

16th. Rosecrans concentrates his army, about 48,000, on the West Chicamauga, Georgia, while Bragg is in position on the east side.

19th. *Battle of Chicamauga.*—Bragg, reinforced by Johnston's division and paroled prisoners from Vicksburg, and Longstreet's forces from Va., about 94,000 strong, attempts to flank the left of Rosecrans' army, about 11 A. M., but is finally driven back by Gen. Thomas' forces one and a half miles. At 2 P. M., a strong Confederate force is hurled against McCook and Crittenden, whose forces are broken and driven back, but being reinforced, the Confederates are repulsed and retire; at night both armies occupy about the same position of the morning.

20th. *The Battle of Chickamauga* reopens at eight and a half A. M., by a furious attack by Breckenridge and Cleburne, on the left, under Thomas, but his veteran troops hold their ground in spite of assault after assault. At 11 o'clock Longstreet makes a furious attack upon the Union forces, but is checked; yet he rallies again and again, and finally the Union center and right brake in confusion. Thomas now moves from left to right and forms his forces in the shape of a crescent, at the base of Mission Ridge, being reinforced by two brigades of reserves, and portions of other corps, holds his position against the indomitable courage and repeated terrific assaults of the enemy under Longstreet, who now falls back and leaves Thomas, at night, master of the wellfought field, who now falls back to Rossville. Union loss, in the two-days' battle, 1,644, killed; 9,262, wounded; and 4,945, missing; also, a cavalry loss of 500. Total, 16,351. Bragg's official report gives killed, wounded and missing, 17,000.

20th. Meade advances.

21st. Rosecrans' army falls back to Chattanooga, and Thomas, holding the rear, is attacked, but repulses the enemy ..... The enemy are driven from Orange and Madison Court Houses, Va., Generals Buford and Kilpatrick taking 45 prisoners.

23d. The Unionists defeat the forces of Hampton and Jones, near Madison Court House, Va., killing 50 and capturing 85.

24th. The enemy attack Gen. Palmer's command, near Chattanooga, and are repulsed, with loss, after two hours' hard engagement...... The 12th Army Corps leaves the Rapidan to reinforce Rosecrans.

25th. Mosby's guerrillas defeated at Upperville, Va., and 700 horses and mules taken.

26th. Gen. Holmes succeeds Gen. Price in command of the enemy's forces at Arkadelphia, Ark.

28th. The 20th and 21st corps of McCook and Crittenden consolidated and called the 4th and given to Gen. G. Granger...... The Virginia Confederate House of Delegates unanimously rejects propositions looking toward peace.

29th. Gen. Dana attacks the enemy near Morgan's Bend, on the Mississippi, but repulsed with several hundred killed and wounded and 1,500 prisoners.

October 1st. Sherman's corps moves to reinforce Rosecrans..... Gen. Meade's official report says the loss of the Gettysburg campaign was 2,834 killed, 13,709 wounded, and 6,643 missing ; total, 23,186 : and captured 13,621 prisoners, 3 guns, 41 standards, and 24,978 small arms.

2d. 4,000 Confederate cavalry, under Wheeler, attack McMinnville and capture the 4th Tenn., infantry, burning a locomotive and ten cars.

4th. Col. McCook overtakes Wheeler's cavalry at Anderson's Crossroads and defeats and drives him ten miles, killing and wounding 120, taking 87 prisoners, 500 mules and a large quantity of United States stores.

5th. An unsuccessful attempt to blow up the new ironclads in Charleston harbor by torpedoes.... Marmaduke, with about 2,000 Confederates, makes a raid on southwestern Missouri...... Chattanooga shelled from Lookout Mountain by the enemy.

6th. 85 guerrillas capture 300 Federalists and $4,000 in a raid on Glasgow, Kentucky.

7th. Gen. Green captures 480 Unionists at Morganza, La., but compelled to retire before Gen. Dana's forces.... Enemy capture Shelbyville, Tenn...... The Confederates defeat the Unionists at Como, Tenn., after two hours' contest, killing, wounding and capturing 37...... 300 Quantrell's men, in Federal uniform, attack 100 of Gen. Blunt's staff and body-guard, near fort Scott, capturing and killing 78.

8th. 2,000 Confederates, under Coffee and Shelby, enter Warsaw, Mo., and slaghter men, women and children, indiscriminately. ......*Battle of Farmington, Tenn.*—Gen. Crook defeats Gen. Wheeler, killing and wounding 125, capturing 300. Union loss, 29 killed and 150 wounded.... The enemy burn Carthage, Mo.

....4,000 Confederates, under S. D. Lee, attack 1,500 Unionists, under McCrellis and Phillips, at Salem, Miss., and defeat the Federals after a well contested battle, killing and wounding near 20.

9th. Crook pursues, and comes up with, Wheeler's forces at Sugar Creek, Tenn.; in a running engagement of 15 miles; he captures 500 Confederates and scatters the remainder, taking 1,000 calalry arms.

10th. The Union troops defeat, and drive from the field, 6,000 Confederates at Blue Springs, Tenn.,, capturing 150. Union loss, 100 killed and wounded...... Lee attempts to flank Meade's right, but is checked by Meade advancing against Lee's right...... The Unionists, after a stubborn conflict at Madison Court-house, Va., fall back to Culpepper.... The enemy defeated at Bible Ridge, Tenn., fall back to Henderson.

11th. Gen. Chalmer, with 5,000 Confederates, attacks and drives the garrison into their fortifications at Colliersville, Tenn., but Sherman, with a detachment of the 13th Regulars, arrives during the contest, and, assisting the garrison, defeats and drives the enemy with heavy loss. Union loss, 20 killed, 50 wounded and 20 missing.... Meade retreats from the Rapidan—Lee following.... The enemy driven from Henderson to Bristol, Tenn., with a loss of over 300 killed and wounded in the two days' engagement.

12th. Shelby and Coffee's guerrillas defeated at Boonville, Mo. .... The Unionists defeat Chalmer's forces at Byhalia, after two hours' battle, killing and wounding 50.... Union troops defeat the enemy at Sulphur Springs, Tenn., after about two hours' conflict, losing 40 killed, 100 wounded.

13th. Col. Hatch defeats Chalmer's forces at Wyatt's, on the Tallahatchie, taking 75 prisoners and 300 Confederates.... Gen. Brandon effectually defeats Shelby's guerrillas at Marshall, Missouri, capturing their artillery and most of their train..... 155 men of the 6th and 11th West Virginia regiments defeat after 12 hours' engagement 800 Confederates, killing and wounding about 50.

14th. *Battle of Bristow's Station, Va.*—Gen. A. P. Hill attempts to turn Meade's right flank again, but is prevented by severe fighting of the 2d corps and part of the 5th, under Warren and Gregg, killing and wounding 400 and take 450 prisoners, 2 colors and a battery.... Enemy defeated at Blountsville, Tenn., losing 8 killed, 26 wounded, and 10 captured, and also 3 locomotives and 34 cars.

15th. Meade's forces reach nearly to Manassas.... Grant assumes command of the military division of the Mississippi, embracing the Departments of Ohio, Cumberland and Tenn.

16th. The Army of the Potomac in line of battle.

17th. The Confederate army attempts to cross Bull Run, but

History of the Great Rebellion.

is driven by Federal artillery, losing 100 killed and wounded. Unionists 2 killed and 24 wounded....29 Confederates captured, with horses, arms, etc., by Sullivan's scouts, at Martinsburg, Va.

18th. McPherson, in an engagement with Confederate cavalry at Canton, Miss, captures 200....Lee retreats towards the Rapidan. ....Imboden surprises and captures 500 men, and supplies, at Charleston, Va.

19th. Lee's rear-guard and Buford's cavalry have 4 hours' artillery battle, when the cavalry make a charge and drive the enemy in confusion....Lee's forces cross at Rappahannock Station.... Thomas succeeds Rosecrans in command of the Army of the Cumberland....Kilpatrick, in an engagement with Stuart's Confederate forces, at Buckland's Mills, Va., loses about 100 men.

20th. Lee retreats, and Meade in pursuit....Sherman's advance defeats Wheeler's cavalry at Bristow Station, Va.....The 5th Ohio cavalry defeats the Confederate cavalry at Cherokee Station, Ala, killing 6 and wounding 15, with a Union loss of 2 killed.

21st. Gen. Osterhaus, with 2,500 men of the 15th corps, encounters Loring and S. D. Lee, with 5,000 Confederates at Cherokee Station, Ala. The enemy flee after 1½ hour's fighting, losing 300. Union loss, 100.

22d. Capt. Bunch, with 60 men, defeats 200 of Hawkins' guerillas at Columbia, Tenn., killing 9 and taking 12 prisoners.

24th. Butler to take command of the 18th army corps, and the Department of Virginia and North Carolina.

25th. In a determined engagement, the enemy are driven beyond the Sweetwater, with a loss of over 300. Unionists lost about the same....Marmaduke and Cabell with 4,000 rebel cavalry, attack 700 Unionists under Col. Clayton, but after a stubborn resistance are defeated, losing 300 killed and wounded. Union loss, 11 killed and 33 wounded.

26th. 500 North Carolina and Georgia refugees en route to join the Unionists of East Tenn., are attacked at Warm Springs, N. C. by part of the 25th N. C. regiment, but are defeated with 6 killed and 30 wounded....Forts Sumter, Moultrie and Johnson bombarded.

27th. Gen. W. T. Sherman to command the Department of Tenn....Shelby's guerillas driven out of Mo......Greek fire thrown into Charleston, from the batteries on Morris' Island.

28th. Col. Caldwell, with 700 Unionists, takes Arkadelphia, Ark., driving out and capturing several hundred rebels.

29th. A severe battle between Hooker and Smith's forces, and the enemy under Longstreet, at Brown's Ferry, Tenn., near Lookout Mountain, lasting from 2 to 4 A. M., when the enemy are routed and driven across Lookout Creek, losing in killed, wounded, and missing, over 1,000 and 1,000 Enfield rifles. Union loss, 76 killed, 33 wounded, 22 missing....The 1st Middle Tenn.,

Infantry, under Gen. Stively, attacks & defeats Hawkin's guerrillas at Piney Factory, Tenn., and also at Centreville, with a loss of 20 killed and 66 wounded.

30th. In a Union meeting at Fort Smith Ark., it was resolved, "That Arkansas should be a free State after the war."

Nov. 3. *Battle of Grand Coteau, La.*—1,600 Unionists, under Gen. Burbridge, are attacked by 7,000 Confederates under Dick Taylor and Greene. The Unionists are driven a mile, but being reinforced by McGinn's division, now wheel and rout the enemy, killing and wounding 120, and taking 200 prisoners. Federals lost 26 killed, 124 wounded, and 566 missing.... Hatch's forces repulse Chalmers rebels in an attack on Colliersville, Tenn.... 120 men of the 13th Michigan Infantry, under Maj. Fitzgibbon, overtake and defeat in a stubborn hand to hand encounter, the combined guerrilla forces of Kirk, Cooper, Williams, and Scott, near Laurenceburg, Tenn., killing 8, wounding 7, and capturing 24. Union loss, 3 wounded and 8 horses killed.

4th. *Brownsville, Texas.*—Banks' forces land and occupy the town and Fort Brown, the Confederates having fired and evacuated both places.

6th. Gen. Duffie's cavalry attack and defeat the enemy under Gen. Patton at Lewisburg, Va., killing and wounding 350, taking 3 guns, 100 prisoners and a quantity of small arms.... Averill's cavalry defeat the rebels under Jackson at Droop Mountain.... North Carolina Unionists defeat a Confederate force at French Broad River, N. C.

7th. The enemy under Gen. Williams, 3,500 strong, kill, wound and capture 530 of the 2d Tenn. infantry and the 7th Ohio cavalry, 4 guns and 36 wagons at Rogersville, Tenn., and retreat... Gen. Meade advances from Cedar Run. The 5th and 6th corps under Gen. Sedgewick cross the Rappahannock at Rappahannock Station. The 1st, 2d, and 3d corps under Gen. French, at Kelly's Ford, after a severe and stubborn engagement, the enemy's rifle pits are taken. Union loss 370. Enemy's loss 100 killed 300 wounded, and 1,950 prisoners, 4 pieces of artillery, 2,000 small arms, 8 battle-flags and 1 bridge train.

8th. Skirmishing and fighting in Meade's advance along the south side of the Rappahannock. The enemy crosses the Rapidan. ....Meade occupies Culpepper, Va.

9th. Meade's forces take 700 prisoners near Culpepper, Va .. The Unionists defeat the enemy on the Little Tenn., killing 50 and taking 40 prisoners.... Enemy makes a raid on Bayou Land, Ga.

10th. The 3d Indiana and 8th Illinois cavalry under Col. Clendenning, attack and defeat the Confederate Infantry near Culpepper, Va., killing 9 and wounding 11. Union loss, 3 killed and 8 wounded.

11th. Enemy concentrating on the south bank of the Rapidan.

12th. Plot to burn the Northern cities and release the prisoners on Johnson's Island discovered, among the Confederate refugees of Canada.

14th. Confederate Government places Gen. Johnston in command of Bragg's army....Longstreet advances against Burnside, who falls back toward Knoxville. Skirmishing all day, each side losing about 250 men.

16th. *Battle of Campbell's Station.*—The battle lasts from late in the morning until dark ; Union loss, 250 killed and wounded.

17th. *Knoxville besieged.*—Longstreet advanced on Knoxville. Burnside formed a line of battle around the town, and heavy skirmishing took place.......Gilmore occupies Seabrook Island..... Arkansas City, Texas, surrenders to the Union forces ; 100 prisoners and 3 guns taken.

18th. Fight renewed at Knoxville. Losses yesterday and to-day about 150 killed and wounded....Gen. Ransom's forces capture a Confederate fort at Mustang Island, Texas, without the loss of a man.

19th. Fighting still going on at Knoxville, but Burnside regarded safe.

20th. Federals capture nearly the entire 6th Texas cavalry, at Vermillionville, La......Mosby's band, in Federal uniform, attempt to capture the Unionists at Bealton's Station, but are detected.

21st. Meade's forces occupy Madison Court House, Va.

22d. Severe artillery conflict between Forts Wagner and Gregg, and rebel batteries Beed and Simkins, and Forts Johnson and Moultrie....Sumter and Charlston continue to be bombarded. ....Longstreet still invests Knoxville and part of the city burnt.

23d. Granger at Chattanooga carries the rebel rifle pits, and Bald Knob, half way to Mission Ridge, and captures 200 men ; Unionists lost 111 killed and wounded....Gen. Hooker moves up Lookout Valley, assaults and turns the rebel left, driving them into their works on the Summit.

25th. Bragg evacuates Lookout Mountain, and Hooker takes possession.... *Capture of Mission Ridge.*—Sherman takes two hills, but is repulsed from the third, and moves toward Bragg's rear. Bragg masses against him from the centre. Hooker moves along the Rossville road to Bragg's left, and Grant hurls Thomas' forces against his centre, and carries the rifle pits at the base of the mountain, and then charges up the hill, driving the enemy toward Ringgold. Union loss, 500 killed and 2,500 wounded. Bragg's loss, 2,000 killed and wounded, 7,000 prisoners, 62 pieces of artillery, and 7,000 small arms.

26th. Bragg's retreating forces pursued by the Unionists...... Hooker enters Ringgold......Sherman crosses the Chickamauga and captures 500 prisoners, 4 guns and pontoons.

27th. Bragg's forces demoralized and retreating on Dalton.

Dec. 1st. Hooker evacuates Ringgold, after burning mills, bridges, etc.

2d. Foster's cavalry repulse Longstreet's cavalry on Clinch River, Tenn., and capture 2 guns.

3d. Hardee succeeds Bragg in command of the Confederate forces of Northern Georgia..... Sherman's cavalry reaches Knoxville.

7th. Sherman given command of the Union forces of East Tenn.

8th. President Lincoln issues Amnesty Proclamation to all rebels who will lay down their arms, and thanks to Grant and army for late victories in Tenn.

11th. Fort Sumter bombarded.

15th. Bombardment of Charleston continued.

17th. 1,600 Confederates repulsed in an attack on Fort Gibson, Indian Territory.

20th. Lee's army in winter quarters.

25th. Charleston shelled with 200-pounders, and fired in several places. The city is almost deserted by the citizens.

27th. Gen. Johnson takes command of the Confederate forces at Dalton, Ga.

31st. Union troops under Col. McChesney, rout a party of rebels at Washington, N. C., capturing 10 men, 1 gun and caisson. Union loss, 1 killed, 5 wounded.

1864.

January 1st. A scouting party of 75 men under Capt. Hunter, attacked near Rectortown, Va., by a force of 500 to 700 cavalry. The Unionists fought until 56 of their party were either killed or captured, the others fled to Harper's Ferry.

3d. Sam Jones, with 4,000 men, capture 280 Unionists, after a brave resistance, near Jonesville, Tenn.

6th. Lieut. Greble, with a detachment of Unionists, en route for Fort Smith, is attacked by the rebel Col. Hall, and 9 of his men captured.

7th. Unionists defeated losing 200 men, at Bean Station, Tenn., after 4 days' skirmishing.

10th. Major Cole's battalion attacked by Mosby with 400 men, on Lincoln Heights, Va.; after an hour's hard fighting, Mosby was defeated, leaving his dead and wounded. Unionists, 2 killed, 11 wounded.... Bombardment of Charleston continues, half the city destroyed.

15th. 1,000 barrels and boxes have been sent to Union prisoners in Richmond, from Baltimore.

17th. The garrison at Fort Morgan revolt and hoist the Union flag, and attack and drive off the gunboats. Troops sent from

Mobile subjugate all the garrison, but 4 who escape. 70 of the leaders condemned to be shot.

18th. The enemy secures 500 wagons, 800 cattle; several hundred barrels of flour, and other stores abandoned by Gen. Sturgis, at Strawberry Plains, who falls back in the direction of Knoxville.

20th. The Mobile Enquirer states there are 200,000 stragglers from the rebel army.

22d. The enemy advances against Pine Bluff, in three columns, commanded by Marmaduke, Fagan and Shelby; Marmaduke attacked, but stands his ground; Fagan is defeated; Col. Clayton marches 40 miles in 24 hours, defeates Shelby's division of 800 men, driving them 7 miles.

27th. Longstreet's advance attacked Gen. Sturgiss yesterday, at Fair Gardens, Tenn. He fell back to a good position and opened on the enemy at daylight this morning; the battle rages till 4 P. M., when the enemy yields, with 65 killed and wounded, 100 prisoners, and 2 rifled guns.

29th. Col. Snider, with a train of 80 wagons, escorted by 800 men, is defeated by 2,000 rebels near Williamsport, Va., losing most of the train.... Col. Hamilton, with 500 rebels, captures the garrison of 150 men at Scottsville, Kentucky, after a desperate fight.

February 1st. *Attack on Newburn, N. C.*—Early this morning, the rebels, said to be 15,000 strong, attack the Federal outposts 8 miles from Newburn; the Union forces yield to superior numbers, destroying their camp, and losing near 30 killed and 200 captured, with some artillery and 300 small arms; at the same time the rebels are defeated on the south side of Trent River, losing 35 killed and wounded.... Capt. Shoemaker, with 75 men, defeats 40 of Forrest's pickets near Lagrange, Tenn., drives them 4 miles, having 2 killed, 1 wounded, and 10 captured; Unionists, one *horse* wounded.

2d. The enemy attack Newburn, N. C., capture and destroy the Union gunboat "Underwriter," and also defeat a force of Federal cavalry in sight of Fort Trotten.

4th. *Skirmish at Satatia, Miss.*—Col. Coates, with a detachment of Sherman's command, sent against Yazoo City.... At Satatia, 3,000 Texans fired at the transports. The land forces, assisted by the gunboats succeeded in dislodging the enemy.... Gen. Sherman had a skirmish with the enemy at Champion Hills, Miss.; 15 killed and 30 wounded.

5th. Col. Coates' expedition occupies Yazoo City, Miss.

7th. Dick Taylor, with 3,000 troops, attacks the Union forces opposite Natchez, Miss., but are foiled and driven 6 miles.

8th. Gen. Dick Taylor renews the attack on the forces near Natchez, but is again repulsed.

9th. 109 Federal officers escape from Richmond.

12th. Gen. Sherman narrowly escapes capture by a charge of 200 rebels.

14th. The garrison of 200 colored troops at Waterproof, La., attacked by 800 rebel cavalry; by the aid of the gunboats, after 2½ hours' fighting, are driven off; Union loss, 2 killed and 5 wounded; rebel loss, 8 killed and 5 prisoners.

15th. Col. Gallup, with 400 picked men, surprise and in 3 minutes put to flight the whole force of Col. Ferguson's 16th Va. 16 rebels killed and many wounded; Col. Ferguson and 60 others, and 80 stand of arms captured; 1,600 Union prisoners released; Union loss, 0.

16th. A picked company of men under Capt. Marshall, made a forced march from Barbers', Fla., to Gainsville, Ga., surprise the guards and gave the contents of the Confederate store houses to the poor.

19th. Gen. Grierson destroys over 100,000 bushels of corn for the enemy.

20th. *Battle of Olustee, or Ocean Pond, Fla.*—Gen. Seymour, with 5,000 men in 3 divisions, commanded by Cols. Burton, Montgomery and Hawley, meets the enemy 13,000 strong, within about 5 miles of Olustee. A division of Hawley's brigade receives the first fire; equipped with inferior guns, are unable to return the same; the left wing of the regiment broke, not, however, till 350 of their number are disabled. The enemy then moves upon the right under Burton, who fought gallantly till the fall of several officers causing confusion, when they fall back with the loss of 2 guns. The Union troops retreat from this unequal contest, followed closely by the enemy, but without avail. Rebel loss, 150 killed, 900 wounded; Union loss, in all, 1,200.

23d. Farragut shells Fort Powell, near Mobile, all day, with 6 monitors and 4 gunboats.

24th. Jeff Davis appoints Gen. Bragg Commander-in-Chief of of the Confederate armies.

25th. Several skirmishes to-day....Gen. Smith's expedition destroys over 1,000,000 bushels of corn, and captures 1,500 mules and horses, 2,000 negroes, and 300 prisoners....Farragut still bombarding Fort Powell.

March 1st. Kilpatrick's cavalry, 5,000 strong, within the outer fortifications of Richmond, and shell the city. A detachment of this command under Dahlgren goes to Frederick Hall Station, and captures 12 officers. It is said Gen. Lee narrowly escaped capture; also cut the telegraph wire and destroyed the railroad.

2d. Kilpatrick defeats a strong force, and destroys Lee's communication with Richmond....Gen. Custar returned, having penetrated to within 3 miles of Charlottesville, in Lee's rear. He repulsed Stuart, capturing 50 prisoners and 300 horses....Butler sends a party to look after and assist Kilpatrick.

4th. Custar makes another successful raid.... Free State Government of Louisiana inaugurated.

5th. President Lincoln orders the sentence of death against deserters to be imprisonment during the war.... Several skirmishes to-day.

6th. 23 Union soldiers hung at Kingston, N. C., as deserters from rebel conscription. They met their fate with great fortitude.

8th. Lincoln presents in person Gen. U. S. Grant his commission as Lieutenant General of the army of the U. S.... 700 prisoners exchanged for an equal number of rebel prisoners, at City Point. ....The expedition for Red River loading at Vicksburg.... A scouting party returned to Madisonville, La., having cleared the country of guerrillas; and also the 9th and 10th Louisiana cavalry, capturing 10 prisoners, arms, horses, blood-hounds, and 30 negroes.

9th. The House of Representatives passes a vote of thanks to Gens. Rosecrans and Thomas, for gallantry at Chickamauga.... Gen. Banks leaves New Orleans to take immediate command of the Red River expedition.

10th. Gen. Franz Sigel assumes command of the Department of Wheeling.... Gov. Brown, of Ga., in his message, shows a want of confidence in the Jeff Davis Government.... The Richmond Examiner urges the immediate execution of all prisoners taken of Dahlgren's raid, and that it is time to raise the black flag.

11th. Sherman's expedition, including Smith's, sums up about as follows: destroyed 150 miles railroads, 67 bridges, 700 feet trestle, 20 locomotives, 28 cars, 10,000 bales cotton, several steam mills, and over 2,000,000 bushels of corn. Upwards of 8,000 refugees came in with the several divisions of the army. Sherman's loss in killed, wounded and missing was only 175.

14th. Gen. A. J. Smith, with 10,000 men, captures Fort De Russy, with 300 prisoners, 8 guns, a quantity of gunpowder, and small arms.

16th. Arkansas, by a vote, becomes a free State..... Skirmishes in Mississippi and Tenn.

17th. Lieut. Gen. Grant assumes command of the armies of the United States.... Disloyal persons in Kentucky attempt to turn the State over to rebel authorities.

20th. Lee's army reported 130,000 strong; total Confederate army, 275,000.

21st. Skirmish 20 miles above Alexandria, La., and at Pilatka, Fla., enemy defeated.

23d. Gen. Steele's command leaves Little Rock for Shreveport, La., with 15,000 men, to co-operate with Banks.... Skirmish at Cave City, Ky.... Forrest, with 5,000 men, on a raid in West Tennessee.

24th. Forrest captures the garrison at Union City, Tenn., consisting of 425 men.

25th. Forrest, with 7,000 men, demands the surrender of the *Fort at Paducah, Ky.* Col. Hicks, in command, refuses ; Forrest at once makes the assault, but fails, he again demands the surrender, promising the treatment due prisoners of war, if at once given up ; but, if compelled to reduce it by assault, he would extend no quarters ; again the gallant Hicks refuses, and repels 3 successive assaults. In the afternoon, 3 Union gunboats arrive, and drive the Confederates out of town. During the shelling of the gunboats, Forrest placed women and children facing the fire in front of his lines, some of whom were killed and wounded. The firing ceased at 10 o'clock ; Union loss, 12 killed, 40 wounded ; enemy's loss, 300 killed, 1,000 wounded. The rebel Gen. Thompson was among the slain.

30th. A detachment of Steele's forces attacks the enemy 1,000 strong, at Monticello, Ark., defeating them.

April 2d. Grierson's cavalry defeated by Forrest at Sommerville, Tenn., with a small loss....Steele's rear-guard under Rice is attacked by Shelby's force of 1.200 cavalry, and 2 guns, near Elkin's Ferry, Ark. Enemy repulsed with a loss of 100 killed and wounded ; Union loss about the same....Skirmish at Crump Hill, La.

3d. Skirmish at Barrancas, Fla. Confederates lost in all, 30 ; Union, wounded, 3.

4th. The Union troops under Steele, near Elkin's Ferry, Ark., attacked by Marmaduke with 2,500 cavalry, and five pieces of artillery ; after hard fighting, the enemy withdrew, loss on both sides about 100 killed and wounded ;...House of Representatives pass resolutions affirming the Monroe doctrine.... Capt. Phelps, of gunboat No. 26, captures a mail-bag of 500 letters from Richmond, and 60,000 percussion caps for Price's army.

8th. *Battle near Mansfield, La., Disaster to the Union Arms.* The expedition of Gen. Banks up Red River, with 14,000 men, under the immediate command of Gens. Franklin and Smith. Near Mansfield the road leaves the river, and support of the gunboats, running through a heavy pine forest. The advance consisted of over 300 cavalry wagons, protected by an insufficient cavalry force, several miles in the rear was the nearest infantry support. While in this forest, the advance falls an easy prey to the lurking foe. A small brigade of infantry sent up, was soon defeated by Dick Taylor, the rebel commander. Then another is sent into action, but are equally unfortunate ; the 4th division then engage the enemy about 5,000 strong. The enemy now mass their whole force, 10,000 strong, upon these, and cut them up severally, leaving no alternative but immediate retreat ; soon confusion ensues, terminating in a fearful panic, wildest confusion reign. "Let every man take care of himself," is the cry, and when thus driven some four miles, they encounter the 19tn corps,

7,000 strong, under the supervision of Banks and Franklin, who put forth every exertion to stay the disorderly retreat but without success. The presence of this force hold the enemy somewhat in check. The retreating forces fall back 12 miles to Plesant Hill, where the forces combine to meet the advancing foe. Banks' loss was 2,000 out of 8,000 on the field, the enemy greatly outnumbered him. The wagon train was sent forward against the advice of Franklin and Ransom.

9th. *Battle of Pleasant Hill, La.*—At 4 P. M., the enemy under Dick Taylor made an assault in overwhelming numbers against the loyal troops, who were driven step by step up the slope of a hill, after the most obstinate resistance; just behind this crest lay the Union reserve, who pours into them such a withering fire as to cause them to recoil in disorder; this is followed by a bayonet charge, resulting in the rout of the enemy, and the recapture of 8 guns. Inferior in numbers, fall back to *Grand Ecore*. Gen. A. J. Smith by his valor saved the army from annihilation. On both sides there has been over 6,000 killed and wounded in the two battles.

11th. The ill-fated army of Banks reaches *Grand Ecore*, 35 miles from Pleasant Hill, our entire loss at this date 670 killed, 4,200 wounded and prisoners, 30 guns, over 400 wagons and teams. The enemy captured a quartermaster's safe, containing $1,000,000.

12th. *Confederate Disaster at Blair's Landing.*—In consequence of Banks' defeat, Porter's fleet of 12 war vessels moves down Red River. The iron-clad "Osage" ran aground at Blair's Landing. She was attacked by over 2,000 dismounted cavalry, commanded by Major Gen. Green. Two cannon, together with 2,000 muskets, are discharged upon the iron monster, but their contents prove as harmless as a shower of hail. The "Osage" belches forth death, with terrible effect, defeating succe-sive charges from the deluded foe. The "Lexington" now steams into action, giving a terrific cross-fire, repelling the vaunting foe with a loss of 500 killed and wounde l, and Green among the slain.

The enemy under Gen. Buford, demand the surrender of Columbus, Ky., held by Col. Lawrence, promising white soldiers the treatment due prisoners, and to return colored soldiers to their masters, but if carried by storm no quarters. Such terms could not be accepted. In this extremity, a number of returned soldiers and a battery pass in hailing distance on the river, and soon compell the foe to flee....*Skirmish at Painsville, Ky.*—1,000 rebels engage 700 Unionists under Col. Gallup; at the first assault, the Unionists fall back to a stronger position. from which the enemy are soon compelled to flee, leaving 50 prisoners and 100 horses.

MASSACRE AT FORT PILOW.—The garrison consisted of about 550 Federal troops, 260 being colored. On the 12th the rebels under Forrest approach the fort; at sunrise the pickets are driven in, at 3 P. M. the rebels having failed thus far, resorts to the flag of truce. They first demanded the surrender of the fort, to which Major Bradford replied, asking one hour to march out. Immediately a second flag of truce comes with communication if not surrendered in twenty minutes an assault will be made on the fort. To this the Federal commander demurred. While the flag of truce is flying, the rebels creep into a position where they can overwhelm the garrison by assault. Capt. Marshall of the gunboat sees their maneuvering, but will not violate the flag of truce by firing. Immediately the fort is captured. Now transpires a scene too horrid to contemplate. The garrison having thrown down arms, they indiscriminately murder men, women, and children, not sparing the sick in the hospital. This scene only needs the "tomahawk and scalping knife to exceed the worst attrocities ever committed by savages." From 300 to 400 are known to have been killed; some 300 in cold blood.

14th. At 2 P. M., the enemy again demands the surrender of Paducah, Ky., receiving a rejoinder, approaches the Fort, 800 strong, but retreats after a short fire, and carries off considerable plunder belonging to citizens.

16th. The enemy under Mosby, 800 strong, demands the surrender of Bristow Station, Va., capturing 25 pickets. Gen. Grant narrowly escapes capture.

17th. An armed party of poor women appear in the streets of Savannah, Ga., demanding "bread or blood," seizing all the bread they could find, but suppressed by the military.

18th. Thirty rebel ironclads ready for action.

20th. The Federal garrison under Gen. Wetzel, 2,000 strong, holding Plymouth, N. C., after several days' assault capitulate to the enemy. The rebel gunboats were of effective service in the battle. Union loss, 150 killed and wounded. Some shot after surrendering. This is a serious loss to our occupation of this part of North Carolina. Rebels under General Hoke 10,000 strong.

23d. The enemy closely press Gen. Banks' retreating army from Grand Ecore to Alexandria.

Battle at Cane River.—An obstinate battle of three hours, in which the over-confident rebels are defeated. Enemy's loss, about 400 men, and 9 pieces of artillery; Banks' loss, 400 killed and wounded.

25th. The rebel Col. Drake, with a superior force, captures a train of 200 wagons, 4 guns, and nearly 2,000 men, near Pine Bluff, Ark.

26th. The gunboat "Eastport," of Porter's fleet, ran aground 50 miles above Alexandria. Porter resolved to blow her up. At this instant a concealed enemy opened a fire of 1,200 muskets, attempting to board the Cricket, but being severely handled, fled, when the Eastport is blown up by 2,000 pounds of powder. The fleet then passes unmolested to a point 20 miles above Cane River, where they came in contact with 18 guns.

27th. $440,000 awarded the crew of the Federal steamer "De Soto," as their just division of 2 blockade runners captured as prizes.

28th. Admiral Porter, after a series of disasters, from the enemy's batteries and musketry, almost miraculously arrives at Alexandria, Va.

29th. Major Gen. P. H. Sheridan commissioned Chief of Cavalry of the Army of the Potomac.

30th. The Fourth Auditor's office distributed $506,000 of prize money, and settled 3,299 prize claims during this month.

May 1st. Porter with a large force is engaged in constructing dams to carry the boats over the falls at Alexandria, La. Col. Baily engineer.

2d. Gen. Sturgiss routs Forrest, who burns bridges, etc., in his retreat.

3d. Commodore Charles Wilkes reprimanded and suspended from duty for 3 years, for disobeying orders.... Soldiers pay increased from $13 to $16 per month.

4th. Lieut. Gen. Grant's great army, with 6 days' rations, crosses the Rapidan. The 2d corps is commanded by Hancock, 5th by Warren, 6th by Sedgwick, and the 9th by Burnside.

5th. *Battle of the Wilderness, Va.*—The Union forces, 150,000 strong, while moving through the Wilderness, Spottsylvania county, with a solid front, encountered an intrenched enemy, 100.000 strong, under Lieut. Gen. Lee; a battle ensued with a loss of over 12,000 on both sides. Gen. Lee, true to his old tactics, masses heavy columns on our most available points, with great success at first, capturing 1,200 prisoners, but soon paid dear for such strategy. The day passed with no available results, except that Grant secured a slightly better position, learned the position of the enemy, etc... Simultaneous with Grant's move on Richmond, the Army of the Northwest, under Major Gen. W. T. Sherman, commenced its campaign through Georgia. The rocky-faced barriers of Dalton was the objective point.

Disastrous Retreat of Gen. Steele to Little Rock, Ark.—This was occasioned by the disaster of Gen. Banks, with whom he was to co-operate at Shreveport, La. The forces of Price, Fagan and Marmaduke combined to destroy those of Gen. Steele, at Jenkins' Ferry ; he fell back in great haste, destroying the bridges in his rear ; the main body barely escapes annihilation, losing in this campaign 3,000 men, 700 wagons, and 15 pieces of artillery. The enemy lost Gens. W. R. Scurvy and H. Randall.

6th. *Battle of the Wilderness, continued.*—Lee's old tactics of throwing his whole force first upon one wing, and then on the other, was renewed to-day sometimes to his disadvantage, and sometimes with success, as when he captured the brigades of Seymour and Shaler, with their commanders. These severe tactics at one time imperiled the safety of the whole army. After this late in the day, the bravery of Sedgwick's command regained our front and forced the enemy back. Owing to the nature of the ground, no artillery used. This engagement more bloody than yesterday. Grant's loss, nearly 20,000 men. Gen. Wadsworth killed.... Gen. Butler's command lands at City Point, Va.... Gen. Beauregard, with 3,000 men, reinforces Lee.

7th. Lee moves southward for the better security of the Confederate capital. The guns were brought to their position during the night, but firing ceased when the foe retired. Under a general order, the army moves forward to Spottsylvania Court House. Here the enemy are found within their intrenchments.... Gen. Brooks, of Butler's Department, moves upon the Richmond and Petersburg Railroad, burnes the railroad bridge, destroys the track, and has a severe contest with the enemy. 260 killed and wounded.

8th. Grant's army advances south, but subject to constant checks from the enemy. At Tod's tavern, the enemy engage 3 divisions, aided by 2 batteries. Our loss, 350 killed and wounded.... Gen. Kautz's cavalry arrives at Butler's headquarters from Suffolk, having cut the Weldon Railroad, and destroyed a large amount of stores, etc., loss, 45..... Gen. Sherman with 99,000 men, advances on the enemy's position at *Buzzard's Roost Pass*, defended by 55,000 men under Joe Johnson; several days severe skirmishing, makes it apparent that the fortifications of Dalton are impregnable to an assault in front. Sherman's loss in killed and wounded, 800. Johnson loses about 650.

9th. *Grant's advance continued.* In crossing River Po, a spirited engagement takes place, between some divisions under Hancock, Birney and Gibbons. Grant is encircling the Confederate forces at Spottsylvania Court House. Our troops withstand the enemy's assaults with marked bravery. The losses are heavy. The gallant Sedgwick is picked off by a sharp-shooter, engulfing the whole army in gloom. In some parts of the field, our troops are the assailants. At night our troops fall back and the enemy are still in possession of their strongholds..... *Gen. Butler's co-operating movement....* Gens. Q. A. Gilmore and W. F. Smith, advance in force, and cut the railroad 6 miles from Petersburg, and 13 from Richmond, crippling Lee's supply.... Gen. Sheridan, with 8,000 cavalry, has accomplished his celebrated raid around Richmond, and destroyed 1,500,000 rations for the Confederate army.

10th. *Battle of Spottsylvania Court House, Va.*—A sanguinary battle without decisive results. The lines of battle six miles; the enemy's breastworks extend nearly the same distance, protecting Spottsylvania Court House. The artillery, dormant for several days, used with marked effect. The enemy gives back slowly, but not without losing 4,000 killed and 8,000 wounded on the field. Gens. J. C. Rice and T. G. Stevenson among the slain. The loyal army is now 15 miles south of the battlefield of the Wilderness.

11th. The day spent in a series of manœuvres to deceive the enemy as to the design of to-morrow. Constant cannonading to prevent his fortifying. The Confederate Gen. Longstreet wounded. Grant, in to-day's report, says: "I propose to fight it out on this line, if it takes all summer." Total number of prisoners to this date, 5,000, killed, wounded and missing, about 32,000....Gen. Sheridan in a raid, is intercepted at Yellow Tavern, by J. E. B. Stuart, Chief of Cavalry; a terrible battle ensues, in which the enemy are scattered and Stuart slain.

12th. Grant's army has a hard battle of 15 hours. At daybreak Hancock's forces assail the enemy's intrenchments, and capture by surprise 3,000 Confederates, including Gens. E. Johnson and G. H. Stewart, and 30 guns. The enemy fails in five attempts to regain his lost works, held by Burnside and Warren; at the same time desperate efforts are put forth to assail the enemy's works in a distant part of the line, but without success. Thus the day passed in most determined efforts on the part of the combattants. Our loss near 11,000. We captured 4,000 prisoners.

13th. Gen. Grant's advance—Ninth day. Part of the enemy withdrew in the night. The day stormy. New combinations being effected....A heavy force under Gens. Gillmore and Smith, from Butler's department, captures some of the enemy's outer works of Fort Darling, which command the water approaches of Richmond. 27 Confederate Colonels killed or badly wounded since we crossed the Rapidan.

14th. Tenth day.—Much manoeuvering for strategic points, both armies digging trenches. The Sixth Corps carries by assault a position of the enemy, but fails to hold it. Gen. Mead and staff came near being captured.

15th. Eleventh day.—But little of military consequence; roads almost impassable. *Gen. Butler's co-operating department.* Last evening near the Petersburg turnpike, the enemy advanced upon our lines, but were driven within their works; to-day they sally forth, and engage Heckman's brigade, but are forced back within their entrenchments. Gen. Sheridan makes a successful raid around the north of Richmond.... Gen. F. Sigel with 5,000 men, severely repulsed by overwhelming numbers near Newmarket, Va., losing 762 men, besides 6 guns and 1,000 small arms, burning the greater part of his train. Confederate loss, total 1,000.

Severe Battle at Resaca, Ga.—Joe Hooker, after fighting 2 days, compells Joe Johnston to flee his stronghold at Resaca. Unionists killed, 700. Rebels not reported.

16th. *Butler's Department.* — Gen. Beauregard, with about 20,000 men, attacks the Union troops of about the same number, at Drury's Bluff, near Fort Darling, driving them back 2 miles. Heckman's brigade nearly annihilated, the commander and many of his men captured. Our loss over 5,000, but would have been greater but for the valor of Gen. Ames.

18th. Grant's operations in Va. Hancock and Wright, by assault, carry 2 lines of rifle pits ; finding the enemy intrenched behind an impassible line of fallen trees, retire. Burnside at another part of the field assails this impenetrable abattis, and also falls back. These assaults cost nearly 1,800 men.

19th. *Grant's Army.*—An effort to flank Lee, but foiled by the movement of the Confederate Gen. Ewell, to intercept our communication with the base of supplies. Gen. Tyler's artillery division, armed as infantry, rescues from him the train of wagons seized. A part of the 2d, 5th, and 6th Corps are brought into action to secure the base of supplies. Our loss, 1,500 men. Confederate loss, 2,000.

21st. *Grant's Movement.*—Owing to the formidable character of the enemy's works, at Spottsylvania Court House, Grant moves for the Confederate Capital, which brings the enemy from his stronghold.

23d. *Battle of North Anna River, Va.*—The army moves direct for the North Anna River. The 2d Corps carries the enemy's works, who arrived the day before from Spottsylvania Court House. At another point the 5th Corps repulses an onslaught of the enemy. Our loss, 1,000 men.

24th. Grant gains the south side of North Anna River, but not without fighting at each ford. Grant's loss 900. Enemy suffered less, but heavily in prisoners.

25th. *Battle of Wilson's Landing, Va.*—Fitzhugh Lee, supported by artillery, demands the surrender of the Wilson's Wharf Fort, on the James' River, garrisoned by negro troops, about 1.200 under Gen. Wild, but is repulsed. After four hours repeated assaults, the enemy abandons the attack. Union, killed and wounded, 40 ; enemy's killed 25, wounded 250, prisoners 11.

31st. Grant reinforced by 2 corps under Baldy Smith..... Warren's corps barely escapes disaster from a part of Ewell's troops ; each commander was engaged in feeling the enemy's position at the time.... Beauregard's losses with Butler to this date 30,000. Entire loss of the United States Army for this month, 60,000.

June 1st. *Battle of Cold Harbor, Va.*—Grant's forces, 125,000 ; Lee's forces 100,000. This battle was bloody and obstinate. We held the field at the loss of 2,500 men, that of the enemy less.

3d. Grant's advance. Another destructive battle near Cold Harbor. Our army makes an attempt to cross the Chickahominy. is overpowered and compelled to retreat, not without serious injury

The enemy in strong position, disputes our passage. Most determined efforts were put forth to dislodge them, but without avail. Our loss, 6,000.

5th. *Battle at Mt. Crawford, Western Va,*—Gen. Hunter, commanding the Union forces, defeats W. E. Jones, and captures 1,300 prisoners in a battle of 10 hours.

6th. *Grant's Army.*—Last night the enemy assaulted the 2d 8th, and 18th corps, but were repulsed with heavy loss. To-day both armies are entrenching within musket shot. At night the enemy attacked part of the 2d corps, and in an hour's battle of fearful carnage is driven back. Total loss around Cold Harbor, 13,153.

8th. *Battle of Petersburg.*—Gen. Gilmore, with 4,900 men, attacks Petersburg. Gen. Kautz storms the first line of defences, and reaches the streets, but falls back for want of infantry support, as previously arranged. Killed and wounded, 30. Disunionists not reported.

10th. *Battle of Guntown, Miss.*—Gen. Sturgis with 8,000 men, defeated by the enemy under Forrest, Lee and Roddy, 10,000 strong, losing 986 killed and wounded, wagon train, artillery, &c. ...Morgan committing severe depredations in Kentucky.

11th. Gen. Hunter defeats McCausland's forces at Lexington, West Virginia....Morgan captures 2 Ohio regiments in Ky.

12th. *Battle of Cynthiana, Ky.*— Gen. Burbridge marches 90 miles in 24 hours, and defeats the raider Morgan in a sanguinary battle of over an hour. Our loss, 150; theirs, in all, 500, 1,000 horses, their week's plunder, and over 100 Ohio troops recaptured.

15th. Gen Grant designs to take Richmond from the south instead of the north side, and lands his troops on the side of the James accordingly.

Sherman's Department.—Gen. Hooker, after a severe engagement, obtains possession of *Pine Mountain.* Gen. Leonidas Polk killed. He was an Episcopal Bishop.

16th. *Battle of Petersburg, Va.*—The assault is led by Hancock, at six o'clock. After 3 hours' destructive battle, and securing some good positions, operations ceased.....Lee reinforced by Beauregard.

17th. *Battle of Petersburg continued.*—At daylight, Potter's division dashes upon the enemy's works, capturing 2 redoubts, with 9 guns and 400 prisoners. Later in the day, Ledlie's division captures a portion of the enemy's works. These are retaken in the enemy's 4th assault. Destructive skirmishes all day. Grant's losses from the 15th to the 18th, about 10,000; Confederates not reported.

18th. Various attempts to carry the enemy's works, but without success. Total loss, 6,000......Hunter, in southwestern Virginia

to the enemy's lines of communications. Union loss from the 5th, 500 men, 7 guns and 600 horses. Enemy's loss unknown.......
Sherman in Georgia.—Extensive skirmishing on the 16th, 17th and 18th at Kenesaw and Lost Mountains. The Confederate position one of complete networks.

19th. The U. S. steamer "Kearsage," Capt. Winslow, captures the Confederate cruiser "Alabama," Capt. Semmes, off the port of Cherbourg, France. The battle lasts less than an hour. The "Alabama" lost 7 killed on board, 17 drowned and 12 wounded. "Kearsage," 3 wounded, one mortally. The vessel scarcely harmed. The "Alabama" destroyed about 80 ships and barks belonging to merchants of the United States, including the gunboat "Hatteras."

22d-23d. An unfortunate move against the Weldon Railroad; nearly 2,500 prisoners captured, with 4 gun batteries, and about 600 killed and wounded. Enemy's loss, not severe.

27th. *Battle of Kenesaw Mountain, Ga.*—The Union forces, 10 brigades, under Sherman, make 2 unsuccessful attempts to assail the enemy's works held by Johnston. Two hours hard fighting proves the enemy's works impregnable. Sherman's loss, about 3,000 killed and wounded. Johnson's loss, 442. Gen. Harker killed.

30th. The celebrated cavalry raiders Kauntz and Wilson, with 7,000 men and 16 guns, after destroying 65 miles of railroad, and inflicting other severe losses upon the enemy; are overpowered and barely escape annihilation. Our loss, 1,200....Sherman occupies Marietta, Ga. The enemy evacuate Kenesaw Mountain during the night.

July 2d. The rebel Gen. Early invades Maryland.

5th. A portion of Early's command takes Hagarstown, robs the stores, and compels the people to pay over $20,000.

6th. Johnson again retreating before Sherman.

7th. Since January 1st, '64, 258 vessels destroyed, worth $12,546,350.

9th. At sunrise the rebel Gen. Early enters Frederick, Md., and exacts $200,000, which is immediately paid. At 9 o'clock he gives battle to Wallace, (4 miles) at Monocacy; overpowered 3 to 2, Wallace falls back with a loss of 1,200 men.

10th. Intense excitement in Washington and Baltimore over Wallace's defeat. The enemy menace Washington, and burn the residence of Gov. Bradford, 5 miles from Baltimore, and plunder various sections.

12th. Gen. Augur completely routs the enemy, who leave 100 of their dead on the field near Silver Spring. Our loss near 280.
....Gen. Rousseau, with 2,700 cavalry, has made a raid of $\frac{2}{3}$ of the State of Alabama, capturing and paroling near 1,000 of the enemy, 100 killed and wounded, 600 horses and mules taken, des

troyed 30 miles of railroad, 13 depots, and captured a loaded train of cars, losing only 50 men.

13th. Early's raid with 20,000 men terminated; he collected vast quantities of stores, and over 4,000 horses.

18th. Grant's line extends 20 miles.

20th. *Battle of Winchester, Va.*—Gen. Averill, in a battle of 2 hours, humiliates the Confederate Early, with 5 000 men, taking 200 prisoners and 4 guns ; total loss, 150 or 200 on either side.

.... *First Battle before Atlanta, Ga.*, at *Peach Tree Creek*—The new Confederate commander Hood, inaugurates new tactics and, at once puts them in execution, rebuking the tardiness of his predecessor, Johnson. He sends out deserters with false reports as to his movements, and makes feints to support these. He dashes upon Sherman's forces just as he crosses the river, before fully formed in line of battle, and sufficiently intrenched, piercing the weakened centre, and comes near severing his army. The indomitable bravery of our men, and some fortuitous circumstances saves us from disaster. Hood gained slight advantages in the morning, but lost them by night, when he falls back to his earthworks, under severe defeat. Hood lost 500 killed, 1,000 wounded, and 100 prisoners. Sherman's loss 1,500.

22d. *Second Battle before Atlanta, Ga.*—During the early part of the day Hood gains some slight advantages, carries some works, but loses them again. The 17 corps furiously assaulted six times. This battle more sanguinary than on the 20th. The enemy finally defeated with a loss of 3.200 killed, 6,000 wounded, 1,000 prisoners, 25 stand of colors, 5,000 muskets. Sherman lost in all 3,722 men, and 10 pieces of artillery.

23d. The movements of the enemy indicate a second invasion of Maryland. This causes a panic and false reports to the effect that Washington is taken, Philadelphia destroyed, &c. In some parts a stampede north..... Gen. Averill, joined by Cook, is defeated at Kernestown by a force dispatched by Early.

24th. The cavalry is precipitated into a disgraceful rout, causing Cook with 8,000 men to fall back. The brave Col. Mulligan killed. 13 officers dismissed for deserting their commands. Our total loss 1,300.

25th. The enemy's cavalry pursue our retreating forces, and occupy Martinsburg. This is the second invasion of Maryland. His loss in the 3 days conflict near that of our own.

26th. *Demonstrations before Petersburg.*—A part of Sheridan's cavalry make a feint on the north of the James, at the same time an assault was in preparation for the enemy's works at Petersburg.

27th. A detachment of our troops carry the position held by Kershaw, and capture 4 20-pounder Parrott guns lost by Butler at

Drury's Bluff. Our loss 50 men.... Unsuccessful Federal raids into Georgia, under McCook.

28th. *Sherman's Third Battle before Atlanta, Ga.*—At first, the enemy under Hood, have some success. In the afternoon the tide of battle changes, and our men repulse every assault. An advance follows, forcing the enemy back, leaving the field in our possession. The battle raged till night. Our loss 50 killed, wounded 439, missing 50. Enemy's loss near 5,000. It is estimated that the enemy has lost in 10 days under their "Fighting General" (Hood) 23,000 men.

30th. *Operations before Petersburg.*—The celebrated mine. 500 feet long, 4½ high, and 20 feet under ground, under one of the enemy's main forts, exploded to-day. Seven tons of powder used. The explosion took place at 4:40 A.M. sending the doomed Fort, with 6 guns and 200 men, high in the air. In terror the enemy rushed from the adjoining forts, fearing a like consequence. In an instant a hundred guns broke forth in a terrific cannonade, to divert the attention from the storming party. Recovering from the shock, in defiance of shells and mortar, he recoiled on the assailants with great determination. To the 9th corps is committed the task of rushing through the opening or crater, for the purpose of carrying the crest of a very strong position, commanding Petersburg. When the troops entered the opening amid the fog of dust and smoke, they paused to throw up hasty entrenchments, exhume the garrison, take out the cannon, etc., instead of storming the crest at once. This brought the disaster of the day, giving the enemy time to recover from the shock, and bring our heroes under an enfilading fire that no mortals could endure; they fell back, with a tumultuous rebound. Supports rushed up, but in vain; repeated efforts were of no avail, and toward noon a retreat was ordered. The crater was little else than a vast slaughter pen. Gen. Bartlett, endeavoring to hold the crater, is captured. It is evident victory was snatched away, when fairly within our grasp. Our loss about 5,000, mostly wounded. Enemy's loss, about 1,200. During the 28th and 29th, a feint on a vast scale was carried on across the James, to deceive the enemy at Petersburg. Some 20,-000 men, with 400 wagons, and 20 guns moved across the Potomac bridge, in the direction of Malvern Hill. To intercept this, Lee hurried from Petersburg with 10,000 men. This was as Grant designed. Late on Friday, nearly all the troops secretly returned to participate in the assault after the explosion of the mine....
McCausland with about 230 Confederates, demands $500,000 of the citizens of Chambersburg, Penn., or they will apply the torch; being refused, they destroy 300 houses, rendering 3,000 people homeless. At noon the enemy left with Gen. Averill in hot pursuit, but succeeded in reaching his reserves..... On the same day, Mosby with 60 men, robs the stores of Adamstown, Md. This

terminates the second raid into Md. The two invasions cost the plundered people $4,960,000.

August 2d. Gen. Kelly defeats B. Johnson and McCausland at Cumberland, and rescues a large amount of their plunder.

3d. A Court of Inquiry is instituted to investigate the cause of the failure on the 30th.....The Confederate Early, with 30,000 men, is in the Shenandoah Valley. Gov. Curtis calls for 30,000 millitia. The enemy defeated on the Jerusalem road. Our loss, 75 men.

4th. The 5 generals and 38 field officers placed under fire at Charleston are released....The enemy in front of Petersburg spring a mine near the 5th corps, it was a failure.....An artillery duel to-day in front of the 18th corps.

5th. The fleet of Farragut moves up Mobile Bay, with the vessels lashed abreast as supports. They soon encountered the enemy's fire. The monitor "Tecumseh" was sunk by a torpedo carrying down 100 of her brave crew, including the gallant Craven. The Confederate gunboat "Selma" captured, and also the ram "Tennessee." At the same time Gen. Granger with the land forces invest Fort Gains in the rear, capturing the water batteries. Our total loss, 50 killed, 100 wounded. During the battle, Admiral Farragut is lashed to the maintop, giving orders through a speaking tube.

6th. A part of the 14th and 23d corps storm the enemy's works near Atlanta, carry the outer line, but failing to dislodge the enemy, fall back....Gen. Averill defeats the raiders at Moorefield, Md., capturing their artillery and wagons, and 500 prisoners. Early's rear-guard left Maryland to-day.....Fort Powell, off Mobile, surrenders to our forces.

8th. Ft. Gaines, consisting of 26 guns, 56 officers, and 818 men, off Mobile, capitulates to the land and naval forces ...Sherman before Atlanta, Ga. Johnson with the 14th corps carries the enemy's works, capturing 175 prisoners. Our loss 25 killed, 275 wounded. Sherman's line extends 14 miles.

10th. The enemy defeats our forces at Gainesville, Fla., capturing 150 prisoners and 100 negroes.

11th. Heavy shelling of Atlanta during last night.... Early continues his retreat towards Strasburg.

13th. Mosby captures at Berryville, Va., 75 wagons, 150 prisoners, 500 horses and 200 cattle.... Gen. Burnside relieved of his command of the 9th corps.... The 2d corps captures near Dutch Gap 500 prisoners and 7 pieces of artillery.

15th. Butler's canal at Dutch Gap shortens the distance of James River, filled with torpedoes 6 miles. By this we flank the enemy's position, bringing us nearer Fort Darling.... The 2d corps ascend the James, and destroys the pontoon bridges 12 miles from Richmond, thus preventing access with Lee, except *via* Man.

chester.... The Confederate Wheeler demands the surrender of Dalton, but is driven out at the point of the bayonet by colored soldiers.

16th. Granger's land forces off Mobile are within 300 yards of Fort Morgan. The ram "Tennessee" opens fire on the Fort.... *Battle of Crooked Run.*—Sheridan captures 300 prisoners from Early, who leaves his dead on the field.... Confederates mining along our works before Petersburg.... Grant's lines within seven miles of Richmond...... Early reinforced. Sheridan falls back and fortifies at Winchester.

18th. The Confederates attack the 18th corps at night, and are repulsed by colored troops. Our loss heavy.

19th. The 5th corps descends and cuts the Weldon Railroad, and then is defeated by A. P. Hill, in a two hours' battle, losing near 4,000 confederate prisoners.

20th. Gen. A. P. Hovey seizes at Indianapolis 400 navy revolvers and 135,000 rounds of fixed ammunition, secreted by rebel conspirators of the Sons of Liberty.... The rebel Wheeler murders the colored garrison at Stewart's Landing, Tenn., and 250 white laborers.... The enemy makes another effort to dislodge the 5th corps reinforced by the 9th on the Weldon Railroad, but are defeated with heavy loss.

21st. Kilpatrick cuts the Macon and Jonesboro Railroad, near Atlanta, capturing a battery, some prisoners, and 2 trains and locomotives.

22d. 32 cases of revolvers seized in New York, intended for the Sons of Liberty.

23d. 50 kegs of powder seized in Terre Haute, Ind., belonging to the Sons of Liberty.... Fort Morgan surrenders to our forces. The garrison 581 sent to New Orleans.... Weldon Railroad destroyed within 4 miles of Petersburg, and 2 miles below Ream's Station.

25th. The enemy again assails Hancock's forces while destroying the Weldon Railroad below Ream's Station; he repels 3 assaults with heavy loss, but afterwards loses 2,000 prisoners, 9 guns, and 3 miles of the road. This road supplies Richmond from North Carolina. Confederate losses for 2 weeks 10,000.... Nine guerrillas and spies shot at Paducah.

26th. Gen. Averill defeats the enemy who attempt to cross into Maryland, with a loss of 80 prisoners.... Sheridan defeats the enemy, killing and wounding 150 and capturing 101 prisoners.

29th. Petersburg furiously shelled.

30th. Grant holds the Weldon Railroad in defiance of Lee.

31st. Gen. Rousseau defeats Wheeler near Nashville, and reopens communication with Sherman.... A detachment of cavalry 1,500 strong under Wheeler, captures Gen. Milligan, with a small force at Lebanon, Tenn.

Sept. 1st. Gen. Mower reinforces Steele at Little Rock ... The 14th corps carries the enemy's works at Jonesboro, capturing 2,000 prisoners, including Brig. Gen. Gorman and 10 guns.... The enemy captures 100 wagons, with supplies, 2 sutler trains, and 640 horses and mules designed for Fort Smith.... Hood at Atlanta destroys his magazine, 7 locomotives, 81 cars, with ammunition, small arms, stores, etc., and retreats south. Union troops occupy Atlanta.

2d. The Mexican Gen. Cortinas drives the enemy from Brownsville, Texas, hoists the U. S. flag, and tenders his services to the Federal commander at Brazos.

3d. National thanks tendered by President Lincoln to Farragut and Canby for signal successes at Mobile Bay. Also, to Sherman for like victories.... Gen. Milroy defeats the enemy near Murfreesboro. They retreat towards Triune.

4th. Gen. Gillam kills Gen. John Morgan, captures his staff, and routs his forces at Greenville, Tenn.

13th. Getty's division of the 6th corps with 2 cavalry brigades, dash upon the enemy on the Winchester road, and capture the 8th S. C. regiment.

14th. Terrific cannonade on Petersburg. Shells reach the city.

17th. The enemy in a dash captures 250 prisoners, and 2,500 reserve cattle opposite Harrison's Landing.

19th. *Battle of Winchester, Va.*—Gen. Sheridan, with nearly 40,000 men, defeats Early, capturing 2,500 prisoners, 5 guns, and 9 battle flags. Confederate Gens. Rhodes, Wharton, Ramsden, and Gordon killed, and Gens. F. Lee, Haines, Ransom, B. Johnson, and Terry wounded. Our loss, killed and wounded, 3,000 to 4,000. Early's loss, killed 500, wounded 5,000.... The draft commenced to-day.

20th Farragut thus far has removed 21 torpedoes from his path to Mobile.... Early retreats to Fishers Hill.

22d. *Battle of Fisher's Hill, Va.*—Sheridan storms the enemy's works, taking 3,000 prisoners and 16 guns. Confederates retreat to Woodstock.... Gen. Forrest captures Athens, Tenn.

24th. Heavy cannonading in front of Petersburg.

26th. Price's army estimated at 10,000. Price captures Ironton, Mo.

28th. *Battle of New Market Hights.*—The 10th corps (colored) carry the Hights at the point of the bayonet. Nearly 200 killed, many wounded.

29th. The 10th and 18th corps take Fort Morris by assault, securing 300 prisoners and 16 guns. Gen, Burnham killed.

30th. The 5th corps carry the first line of the enemy's works at Preble Farm, near Weldon Railroad. Our loss 120. Gen. Welsh killed. After this the 9th corps assault the inner works, and are repulsed with a loss of 500 killed and wounded, and 1,500 prisoners.

Oct, 1st. Kauntz's cavalry reconnoitre within 3 miles of Richmond.

2d. The Confederate Buford repulsed by the garrison at Athens, Alabama.

5th. Hood repulsed by our garrison at Altoona, Big Shanty, and Actworth.

7th. Kautz's cavalry defeated near Chapin's Bluff with a loss of two batteries; afterwards the ground was recovered with heavy loss. Confederate loss, 1,000 in killed and prisoners. Confederate Gen. Gregg killed....Price repulsed at Jefferson City. ....620 exchanged prisoners reach our lines from Richmond.

10th. Col. Hodge with 1,200 men, is defeated by the Confederate Forrest at Eastport, with a loss of 4 guns and 46 killed and wounded.

11th. Col. Weaver, with 90 colored troops, repulses an attack of the enemy 200 strong, five miles below Fort Donelson, Tenn.

12th. Guerrillas repulsed by colored troops at Pine Bluff, Tenn. ....Longstreet and Sheridan fight a draw battle of 3 hours, near Strasburg.

15th. Jeff Thompson with 2,000 Confederates, takes Sedalia, Mo., and plunders the town.

16th. Gen. Sherman takes Ship Gap.

17th. Blunt, with 2,000 cavalry, drives Price from Lexington, Mo....Beauregard assumes command in Sherman's front.

18th. Blunt is driven from Lexington, Mo., by Price.

19th. *Battle of Cedar Creek, Va.*—Gen. Sheridan's army attacked and driven back 4 miles, the left wing routed with a loss of 20 guns. Sheridan returning from Washington, hearing the roar of battle, hastens from Winchester, unites his corps, changes his position, attacks and routs the enemy, capturing 51 guns, prisoners, ambulances, wagons, caissons, etc. Gen. Bidwell killed, with other field officers.

20th. Sheridan pursues and scatters the retreating enemy. At Mt. Jackson 300 wagons captured. Early's entire loss about 10,000 men.

23d. Curtis driven from Westport by Shelby, who in turn is defeated by Pleasanton.

24th. Price defeated near Fort Scott.

26th. Price again defeated, losing 1,500 prisoners, 1,000 stand of arms and 10 guns. Gens. Marmaduke and Cabell, and several Colonels prisoners.

27th. Two brigades of the 18th corps, about to assault the enemy's position on the Williamsburg road, are driven back by a cross fire with a loss of 3,000. Enemy's about 1,500.

28th. Blunt defeats Price with a loss of 450. Union 120.

1865.

January 1st. Capt. N. J. Palmer captures a rebel supply train of 110 wagons and 500 mules......Confederate debt, one thousand five hundred and fifty millions of dollars.

11th. Rosser's Confederate division surprises at 3 A. M., and captures the garrison and Beverly, Va.

12th. Rear-Admiral Porter's fleet of 52 vessels of all classes, 531 guns, leaves Beaufort, N. C., in three columns for Fort Fisher.

13th. Attack on Fort Fisher. Porter's fleet in line of battle at early dawn in three columns. At 7¼ A. M., the forts opened on the fleet; at 8 A. M., the 5 ironclads opened on the fort, over 2,200 strong, at a distance of 1,000 yards. The troops commence to land at 9 A. M. Before 3 P. M., the lines of the 1st and 2d corps open on the fort, and continue till after dark, during which time most of the sea-front guns are dismounted or destroyed, and this part of the fort reduced to a crumbling condition, the entire fleet throwing 4 shells per second. The enemy ceases his fire and shelters in his bomb-proofs before dark. The monitors and ironclads firing at intervals all night. The fort reinforced and strengthened during the night.

14th. Second days' attack on Fort Fisher. From 1 P. M., till after dark, the gunboats, carrying 11-inch, open on the face of the fort to dismount if possible all remaining guns where the assault is to be made, and 2,000 sailors are landed to assault the sea-face and dig rifle pits, under protection of the fleets. Breastworks are also built between the sea and Cape Fear River, and Gen. Terry and Admiral Porter arrange the plan of final assault for to-morrow.

15th. The 3d days' assault on Fort Fisher openes at daybreak, by a terrific fire from the iron vessels and the 11-inch gunboats, under protection of which Ames' forces move to within 150 yards of the fort. At 11 A. M., the entire fleet in three columns, joines in a most terrific cannonade until 3 P. M., changing round to the upper batteries, the gallant assaulting columns bound toward the seaside with great determination, the enemy's main force rallying against them, and the mariners failing to hold the rifle-pits, are compelled to retreat with severe loss. During which engagement Col. Curtis leads around troops, gains the upper parapets, and while the enemy are giving three cheers, thinking they have gained the day, this assaulting force pours in a volley from the rear, and now they struggle for foot after foot, and contend hand-to-hand—giving us one-half of the land front by 5 P. M. Now Abbott swells the assaulting force, and the struggle goes on inch by inch amid terrific carnage and death, until about 10 P. M. After 6½ hours' most gallant and heroic contest, Fort Fisher falls, the most formidable ever taken in the annals of history, and surrendering unconditional about midnight into our hands over 1,800 officers and men, 72 guns, one Armstrong, the camp and garrison equipage and stores, aside from losing in killed and wounded 400. The fleet suffers but little or no damage, but in officers and men severe, losing over 1,000 killed, wounded and missing.

16th. 300 Union troops killed by the explosion of the magazine in Fort Fisher......The enemy blow up Forts Caswell and Campbell, and abandon their works on Smith's Island, and at Smithsville and Reeves' Point, with 162 guns; and also evacuate Fort Smith, near Wilmington.

17th. Gen. Sherman's forces move from Savannah toward Charleston and Branchville S. C.

February 1st. Gen. Sherman's army moving northward very rapidly.

3d. Heavy cannonading on Petersburg.

4th. 3,000 of Sherman's troops from Savannah land on James' Island, two miles from Charleston, while the land forces are nearing the fated city.

5th. Gen. Sherman burns Barnwell, S. C......Advance on Hatcher's Run.

6th. The enemy attempt to drive our forces from their position around Hatcher's Run, bringing on a general engagement along the entire line, and driving back part of our forces with heavy loss.

7th. Hatcher's Run contest renewed with great vigor. While the forces were about equal, the enemy had the advantage in knowledge of the ground, and drove our forces back to their first day's intrenchments. Our loss in killed wounded and missing to date, about 2,000, while the enemy's about 3,000.

8th. The Unionists in a battle at Kinston, N. C. lose 1,500 men and 3 guns. The enemy less.

10th. The assault at Kinston, N. C., renewed. The enemy lost over 2,000 men, the Unionists 500......Gen. Gilmore lands from 3,000 to 4,000 troops on James Island, near Charleston, and drives the enemy from his rifle pits to his main works, leaving their dead, wounded and a number of prisoners.

11th. Siege of Wilmington. Admiral Porter's fleet co-operating in advance with Gen. Terry's land forces, drive the enemy into their works capturing a number of prisoners.

12th. Detachment of Sherman's forces occupy Branchville, S. C.

13th. Gen. Schofield takes Kingston, N. C., after severe fighting.

17th. During last night the enemy about 14,000 strong, evacuate Charleston, S. C., without firing a gun, firing the city in many places, and burning ⅔ of the city, also railroad bridges, immense stores of cotton, arsenals, quartermaster stores, 2 ironclads, and several vessels, and but for the efforts of Union troops, the entire city must have been consumed. At 9 A. M., the identical flag banished in contempt from Fort Sumter on the 15th of April, 1861, streams in glad triumph o'er Sumter and Charleston, while the enemy flees northward from a once proud, but now humiliated city.

18th. At 9 A. M., Major Macbeth surrenders to Gen. Gillmore, the city of Charleston, S. C., with all its forts and defensive works 4,000 prisoners, including 2,000 Confederate deserters found in Fort Sumter, 450 pieces of artillery, 8 locomotives, and much ammunition...... Gen. Sherman's forces occupy Columbia, S. C., and destroy all the enemy's works and stores.

19th. Fort Anderson being under siege for the last two days, by Porter's fleet and 8,000 men under Gen. Schofield, evacuates at dawn, leaving 10 heavy guns, 50 prisoners and ammunition.

20th. Union troops overtake the Fort Anderson garrison, attack and rout them, taking two guns and 340 prisoners...... 200 torpedoes sent from Wilmington down the river, doing however, but little damage.

21st. A party of Confederate cavalry dash into Cumberland, Va., and capture Gens. Crook and Kelly, and their staffs.

22d. Union forces enter Wilmington, being evacuated last night, giving us 19 forts and batteries in all, including those at Wilmington, and down the river ; and also, the largest fortified harbor in the world, and 3 locomotives, 12 cars and railroad stops.

23d. Gen. Terry pursues and captures 700 prisoners.

26th. U. S. Government has captured during the war over 379 vessels, mostly British blockade runners.

27th. Gen. Sheridan leaves Winchester, Virginia, on a cavalry raid.

March 2d. Sheridan, with 8,000 cavalry, defeats the enemy under Early 1,800 strong, at Waynesboro', Va., capturing 1,165 men, 87 officers, 13 flags, 5 cannon, etc.

8th. The greater part of two regiments of Union troops captured near Kingston.

9th. Active skirmishing all day near Kingston ; 200 prisoners captured by the Union troops, but nothing decisive.

10th. The decisive battle before Kingston, N. C., to-day. The loyal forces defeat near 10,000 of the enemy, with a supposed loss of 1,500. Union losses, 500...... Custar's division of Sheridan's command destroys from Feb. 27th, $2,000,000 worth of property.

13th. Gen. Schofield occupies Kinston. Gen. Bragg falls back toward Goldsboro'.

15th. Skirmish with the enemy's advance near Fayetteville.

16th. *Battle of Moore's Cross Roads, N. C.*—Continues all day, Repeated efforts to dislodge the enemy, but not an inch of ground gained.

17th. The enemy abandoned his position during the night, the conflict ceases. Union loss, 747; enemy's loss, 327 killed and wounded, and 273 prisoners.

19th. *Battle of Bentonsville, N. C.*—Sherman's forces engaged, less than 30,000; Johnson's, from 40,000 to 45,000. About noon, in an attempt to turn the enemy's flank, but sallying forth in overwhelming numbers, break the Union line, pressing it back one mile, and capturing 400 prisoners and 3 guns. At 2 P. M., the line is reformed, and order reigns. Shielding behind temporary works they meet another terrible assault of the enemy, repeating the same five times. Although the "fate of the day had trembled in the balance," night falls upon the Unionists holding the field, and nearly 700 prisoners.

20th. *Second Day's Battle.*—The Unionists reinforced, sweep line after line with overwhelming numbers. Johnson, after a determined but fruitless resistance, retreats upon Smithfield. Total Federal loss, 1,646; enemy's loss, about 3,000.

25th. *Battle of Petersburg, Va.*—Gen. Gordon, with 3 divisions of Confederates, surprises and captures Fort Steadman with about 500 men. Turning the guns of the Fort upon the Union lines, he secures the adjoining mortar batteries 9, 10 and 11; at this point his onward rush is checked by the prompt rally of adjacent troops, and amassing the batteries from all quarters, the enemy is pressed back within the Fort, with stubborn resistance, using the captured artillery, and again is pressed beyond, leaving all behind, making the utmost endeavors to regain his lines, but the severity of our guns compel the surrender of 1,758 prisoners...... By 11 A. M., the entire army advances, Wright's 6th Corps and Humphrey's 2d Corps carry the enemy's intrenched picket line; but unable to hold this, fall back. Being reinforced, the line advances and carries the enemy's works amid a terrible musketry and artillery duel, capturing 420. At 2 P. M., the enemy furiously assault the 6th corps to regain his lost works, also at 4½ P. M., the 2d corps, but without avail. Night closes the scene, with victory to the Union forces, and 10 battle flags.

27th. The enemy attack and are defeated by Getty's division. The enemy inaugurate the spring campaign in a disastrous failure. Unionists killed 180, wounded 1,240, missing 990, total 2,410. Disunionists killed and wounded about 2,200, prisoners 2,800, total nearly 5,000.

29th. *Battle of Quaker Road, Va.*—About 3 P. M., Johnson's forces assault Griffin's, Crawford's and Ayers' divisions with great determination, but are repulsed and fall back. Total loss on both sides about 500. During the night a tremendous cannonade broke out, lasting 3 hours, around Petersburg; casualties light.

31st. *Battle of Boydton Plank Road.*—A force of Union troops is ordered forward to secure the strategic position known as Five Forks, but is defeated and driven back. Soon after noon, the enemy attack the brigades supporting the left of Sheridan's lines, who hold their ground. The enemy next drive Davis' brigade from the bridge across Stony Creek, with heavy loss, after this they attack and drive back Sheridan's left centre. Later in the day both armies reinforced, are hurled forth in fearful conflict, charge succeeds charge, but they encounter the entire Federal cavalry; finding it fruitless to attempt to penetrate the Union front, they fall back, and our troops advance. Simultaneous with the above, 2 divisions of the 2d corps dash forward into one of the hottest engagements of the day, the enemy finally withdraw. The day, upon the main, a success to the foe. Our army checked and foiled in her plans. The entire Federal loss from 2,500 to 3,000. The Confederates less. The Federals capture 539 prisoners..... National debt $2,423,437,001.

April 1st. *Battle of Five Forks, Va.*--Gen. Sheridan with 30,000 infantry and cavalry is attacked by the enemy of less numerical strength strongly fortified. At early dawn the enemy succeed in planting their battle flag on the Federal parapets, but are repulsed in a hand-to-hand encounter. With masterly skill Sheridan presses the enemy from position after position, to his main intrenchments, while Grant threatens the whole rebel line. Here they fight with a desperation worthy of a nobler cause, mowing down the advancing columns with fearful slaughter; they waver, stagger and fall back, disaster is imminent. The lion-hearted Sheridan rushes forth in this hour of peril, rallying his brave troops, who again breast the iron storm of death, swarming over the enemy's parapets driving the foe to the rear, and here another dreadful encounter, and the day is won. 4,000 prisoners, 6 cannon, several thousand muskets, ambulance and baggage train, flags, etc., are captured. Federal losses, 2,500 to 4,000. Enemy's loss, 3,000, prisoners added, total amount 7,000.

2d. Jeff. Davis, while in church, receives a dispatch from Lee; stating he can no longer hold the rebel capitol; he flees in the direction of Danville.... Gen. Wilson, with 15,000 men, captures Selma with 2,000 prisoners and 100 guns.

2d and 3d. *Battle of Petersburg and Richmond, Va.*—The artillery opens at 4 A. M., upon the enemy's works of Petersburg, followed by the assault of Getty and Wheaton; at first checked, but regain and carry Forts Welch and Fisher, while Seymour by hard fighting gains the Southside Railroad; also, 2 divisions of the 24th and right of the 2d corps capture 1,000 prisoners and carry the enemy's works to the railroad. The 9th corps carries the strong position of Fort Mahone and adjacent works with 14 guns. The enemy, with a most inveterate determination, make repeated efforts to regain this position, at one time they came near succeeding, but the Federals being reinforced, it passes forever from their grasp. The garrisons now yield to overpowering numbers. The whole line now presses toward Petersburg, another terrible clash of arms, and the spirit-broken foe yields, their commander, A. P. Hill, a pillar of strength, has fallen. In the afternoon, Lee, conscious of his critical position, orders the evacuation of Petersburg and Richmond.

3d. During last night the enemy evacuated Petersburg and Richmond. The 1st Michigan Sharpshooters the first to enter Petersburg. At 4 P. M., Col. Ely's brigade within the city. Trophies too numerous to mention are the result of this victory. At 7 A. M., Gen. Wetzel took possession of the Confederate Capital, greeted by the people. 5,000 stand of arms, 500 cannon, etc., fall into his hands. The fatal stroke to the rebellion has been dealt. Union losses on the 2d and 3d, about 8,000; enemy's not reported, missing about 9,000. Sheridan presses the retreating enemy.

4th, Lee reaches Amelia Court House.... Abraham Lincoln enters Richmond and holds a levee in the rebel Presidential mansion.

5th. Sheridan at Jettersville, and communicates to Grant that he can see no escape for Lee...... Grant is moving in pursuit.

6th. *Battle of Deatonville, Va.*—The 6th corps, with the 2d on its right and the cavalry on its left, at 4 P. M., engage and rout the retreating enemy, capturing many prisoners, 5 General officers, of these Gen. Ewell and Gen. Custis Lee.

7th. *Battle of Barnesville, Va.*—The 2d corps engage the enemy in a spirited combat. Lee after inflicting some loss, retreats on Lynchburg. His position is critical in the extreme. His retreat on Danville cut off. Strong forces flushed with victory almost surround him. His army has dwindled to a small force. The last ray of hope fades in the distance. No casualties given since the 3d.

8th. *Battle of Mobile, Ala.*—Among the chief defences is Spanish Fort, erected by De Soto in 1540, who discovered the Mississippi. A little before nightfall the final preparations are completed. Gen. Canby, with 35,000 land forces, in conjunction with the fleet, of 14 war vessels, etc., commanded by Rear Admiral Thacher, commence the final reduction of the Fort in front and rear, containing about 16,000 troops, under Gen. Taylor, with 5 war vessels. While the heavy siege guns and field pieces mete out destruction, the skirmishers gain a position within the range of their pieces, driving the artillerists from the unsheltered guns. The response of the Fort becomes more and more feeble.

9th. At 1 A. M., the Fort surrenders. At 2 A. M., the Federal troops take possession, capturing 652 prisoners. The others flee by water.

Lee surrenders the Army of Northern Virginia, about 27,000 strong.

12th. At 10½ the Union colors float on batteries Porter and Mackintosh; 4 hours later from the dome of Mobile, the second seaport city of the Confederacy......U. S. losses from March 18th to April 12th, army about 2,500, navy less than 50. Confederates killed and wounded about 2,000, prisoners about 4,000. ......*Battle of Salsbury, N. C.*—Gen. Stoneman with 4,000 cavalry on a raid, defeats Gen. Gardiner with 3,000 Confederate troops who falls back. Stoneman entering the city, captures 1,364 prisoners, 14 pieces of artillery, 1,000 small arms, 1,000,000 rounds of ammunition, and vast military stores.

14th. At 10 o'clock, P. M., President Lincoln is assinated by a pistol shot, and dies April 15th, 22 minutes past 7 o'clock, A. M.

16th. Gen. Upton captures Columbus, Ga., with 1,200 prisoners, 53 guns, and an immense amount of military stores.

17th. Gen. Mosby surrenders his command to Gen. Chapman, at Berryville.

26th. John Wilkes Booth, the assassin of President Lincoln, shot by Sergeant Boston Corbett, in an attempt to flee when commanded to surrender......J. E. Johnson surrenders to Sherman. The Confederate army in North Carolina, about 30,000.

May 9th. Jefferson Davis, the Confederate President, captured at Irwinsville.

12th, *Action of Palmetto Ranch, Texas.*—Between Col. Barrett, with about 400 men, and the Confederates under Gen. Slaughter, about 500 strong, with 3 field pieces, in which 15 were killed and wounded, and 57 made prisoners. Confederates trifling. This is the last action of the war.

SUMMARY.

During 3 years of the war, citizens loaned their government more than two billions.

It is estimated that five hundred millions has been disbursed for the relief of our suffering soldiers, through the Sanitary and Christian Commission and other agencies.

The value of property destroyed by the Federal army, and also by the Confederate army to prevent it from falling into Federal possession, exceeds one thousand millions of dollars.

The aggregate losses by the contending forces, and national debt about eight thousand millions of dollars.

Slave property in 1860, was worth in the United States "$1,976,500,500.

The population of the Loyal States at the outbreak of the rebellion, was 22,342,647; of the Seceded States, 9,103,333. The loyal States were worth $10,957,449,971; the Seceded States, $5,202,176,107.

The following table will exhibit the population and number of men furnished by each loyal State and Territory, to put down the Rebellion, up to 1865:

States.	Population.	Men Fur'd.
California	379,994	14,705
Connecticut	460,147	57,270
Delaware	112,216	13,651
Illinois	1,711,951	258,217
Indiana	1,350,428	195,147
Iowa	674,948	75,860
Kansas	107,206	20,097
Kentucky	1,155,684	78,540
Maine	628,279	71,745
Maryland	687,049	49,731
Massachusetts	1,231,066	151,785
Michigan	749,113	90,119
Minnesota	173,855	25,034
Missouri	1,182,012	108,773
Nebraska	28,841	1,279
New Hampshire	326,073	34,605
Nevada	6,857	216
New Jersey	672,035	79,511
New York	3,880,735	464,156
Ohio	2,339,502	317,133
Oregon	52,465	617
Pennsylvania	2,906,115	366,326
Rhode Island	174,620	23,711
Vermont	315,098	35,246
Wisconsin	775,881	96,118
West Virginia		32,003
Tennessee	1,109,801	29,000
Colorado Ter	34,277	1,702
Dakota Ter	4,837	181
New Mexico	93,516	2,395
Utah Ter	40,273	
Washington Ter	11,594	895
District of Columbia	75,080	16,872

Grand Total 22,342,647.   Total 2,688,523.

56,000 killed on the field of battle: 35,000 died of wounds; 184,000 perished of diseases. Of whites enlisted, one-tenth died in service; of the blacks, nearly one in six.

There was fought about 308 battles; about 100 in Virginia; 39 in Tennessee; Georgia, and Kentucky each 17; North Carolina 19; Missouri 18; South Carolina 10; Maryland 8; Mississippi 21; Louisianna 16; Pennsylvania 2.

Reader, Adieu! May the God, whose dominion is forever and forever, grant peace and prosperity as the continued inheritance of the Great Republic.

www.ingramcontent.com/pod-product-compliance
Lightning Source LLC
Chambersburg PA
CBHW032238080426
42735CB00008B/904